LEARN

SPOKEN

SINHALA

The Most Unconventional
Sinhala Learner's Guide

Second edition

Learn Spoken Sinhala

The Most Unconventional Sinhala Learner's Guide

Sumith Wanni Arachchige

Second edition

I dedicate this book to

My ever-loving nephews Thusitha, Kavindu, Hashitha, Praveen, and Chamod

&

My dear father who left us forever recently and my dear mother without whose strength I would never have had freedom to write

&

My loving little angel Ahasna

Table of Contents

Learn
Spoken
Sinhala

The Most Unconventional
Sinhala Learner's Guide

Preface

I have been asked about my mother tongue, Sinhala (or Sinhalese) by many foreign friends so many times. I also had written some not-so-big grammar lessons personally customized for them. However, I thought of writing some lessons to teach spoken Sinhala in English medium, for lack of (free) resources on the Internet so interested people may find useful.

If you have a good understanding of English language, I am sure you will easily and quickly learn my lessons because I base my teaching of Sinhala sentence structures on English grammar and structures.

Sinhala language is used and spoken by Sri Lankans, and it is the native language of the Sinhalese, the majority race (more 70% of the population) in Sri Lanka. It is more or less the lingua franca in the country. Tamil that is the native language of southern India is also spoken by around 20% in the country.

However, due to racist and antagonistic attitudes of some factions in the society and naive personality of most rulers and policy makers in power, and subservience of the so-called intellectuals, now all the Sri Lankans (initiating from school system) are compelled to learn both the languages – Sinhala and Tamil.

What is the purpose of knowing a language? Have they assessed objectively how multilingualism would affect mass media, education system, and so on in a small geographic area/country like Sri Lanka? Being multi-lingual is in fact a good thing, but that importance or passion should have been felt by each individual. This is lame politics, so I put it aside for now.

This is the second edition of the book. Initially I mainly focused on the content only, but it seemed some readers were not that much happy about the fact that I have taken the simplest layout for the book. Therefore, I have completely changed the layout and formatting of the book.

In this second edition, I have included more examples, dialogs, and practice sentences. I have re-written some paragraphs completely too. I hope this second edition will be easier to read and carry, and of course, it trains you better in mastering the Sinhala.

Sumith Wanni Arachchige
Author

55, Kathuruwatte, Mudungoda 11056
Sri Lanka.

https://www.tekcroach.top
sumithlk@gmail.com
sumith@tekcroach.top

04 February 2020

Introduction

Sinhala has two distinct varieties – Spoken and Written. Spoken Sinhala is much easier and has less strict grammar compared to Written variety.

I am going to write about this spoken variety because it is the variety even the native Sinhala speaker knows and uses daily.

To successfully learn Sinhala or any other language for that matter, you have to do a few things regularly.

> 1. Learn some vocabulary regularly. The more you know the common words, the more productive your language skill will be.

> 2. Learn the fundamental grammar points well. There will be always a little bit more to be learnt however much and long you have been learning. That is not a problem at all.

> 3. Practice regularly what you have learned.

Later, I will show how to write Sinhala letters. It is not difficult because Sinhala is phonetic – that is, there is one-to-one association/map between a sound and a letter. There are 60 letters altogether (but my opinion is only around 40 letters are needed for Sinhala).

Phonetic Aid

Until you learn Sinhala letters (alphabet), I will be using English letters to write Sinhala (this way of writing Sinhala in English alphabet is called "*Singlish*"). To match with the Sinhala phonetically, I am using the following English letters and combinations thereof. I am not using the standard phonetic alphabet for that in my lessons.

A – as in **U**p	**A:** – as in **A**lms
AE – as in **A**t	**AE:** – as in **A**nne
I – as in **I**ndia	**I:** – as in **EA**st
U – as in p**U**t	**U:** – as in b**OO**t
E – as in p**E**n	**E:** – as in l**A**ne
O – as in b**O**ss	**O:** – as in ph**O**ne
K – as in **K**ite	**G** – as in **G**ame
CH – as in **CH**air	**J** – as in **J**ar
T – as in **T**en	**D** – as in **D**avid
TH – as in **TH**ought	**DH** – as in **TH**e
P – as in **P**en	**B** – as in **B**ed
N – as in **N**eck	**L** – as in **L**ake
M – as in **M**ust	**F** – as in **F**an
H – as in **H**at	**SH** – as in **SH**ut
S – as in **S**it	**R** – as in **R**at
Y – as in **Y**et	**V** – as in **V**an
'NG – as in vi**GN**ette	

NOTE:

In Sinhala, there are <u>four</u> special sounds called "sa'ngaka". They are shown below. I use the following technique to denote the sa'ngaka letters.

'ng   **'nb**   **'nd**   **'ndh**

These sounds are not naturally familiar to the English speakers. You just have to listen to those sounds and familiarize yourself. To sound these letters, try this:

"Don't pronounce "n" strongly; just weakly pronounce it while strongly pronouncing the letter after n".

To get an idea of a Sinhala sa'ngaka sound, I will give an example in English. Pronounce "ri_ng_ing". The sound of the underlined part of that word has the sa'ngaka sound of 'ng.

Nouns and Verbs

You know what NOUNS and VERBS are. Nouns denote
something/somebody, and Verbs denote some action.

First, you should learn the following Sinhala verbs and nouns.
Regularly learn more words. We will be constructing Sinhala
sentences mostly using them.

Noun	Meaning
Amma: , Amma	The mother
Tha:ththa: , Tha:ththa	The father
Ayya: , Ayya	The elder brother
Malli: , Malli	The younger brother
Akka: , Akka	The elder sister
Nangi: , Nangi	The younger sister
Gedhara	The house
Pa:ra	The road
Potha	The book
Pae:na	The pen
Bath	Cooked rice
Gasa	The tree
Ka:maraya	The room
Kussiya	The kitchen
Lamaya: , Lamaya	The child
Miniha: , Miniha	The man
Gaehaeni: , Gaehaeni	The woman

Pa:n	bread
Si:ni	Sugar
Vathura	Water
Ae'ndha	The bed
Vaththa	The garden
Kurulla: , Kurulla	The bird
Ira	The sun
Sa'ndha	The moon
A:dharaya	The love
Pettiya	The box
Yahaluva: , Yahaluva	The friend
Sathura: , Sathura	The enemy
Ko:ppaya	The cup
Isko:laya	The school
Pittaniya	The ground
Kalisama	The pair of trousers
Sa:ya	The skirt
Kadaya	The shop
Ispiritha:laya	The hospital
Dhosthara	The doctor
Beheth	Medicine
A'mba	Mango
Anna:si	Banana

You should learn Sinhala nouns in its singular form as much as possible. Singular Sinhala nouns are automatically definite (that is why I have put "the" in front of every English word above). Let us see about plural nouns later.

As you can see, some Sinhala words ending with a long vowel can be pronounced with a short vowel instead (eg. *Amma:* or *Amma*). You should get familiar with different pronunciations.

Following is a list of Sinhala verbs that I recommend you should learn by heart.

Verb	Meaning
Yanava: , Yanava	Go
Enava: , Enava	Come
Kanava: , Kanava	Eat
Dhenava: , Dhenava	Give
Gannava: , Gannava	Take , Buy
Kiyanava: , Kiyanava	Tell/say
Ahanava: , Ahanava	Ask
Balanava: , Balanava	Look
Karanava: , Karanava	Do
Thiyenava: , Thiyenava	Have
Liyanava: , Liyanava	Write
Kiyavanava: , Kiyavanava	Read
Uyanava: , Uyanava	Cook
Venava: , Venava	Become, happen
Laebenava: , Laebenava	Get

Yavanava: , Yavanava	Send
Maranava: , Maranava	Kill
Maerenava: , Maerenava	Die
Naginava: , Naginava	Climb up
Bahinava: , Bahinava	Descend, get off, get down
Baninava: , Baninava	Scold
Natanava: , Natanava	Dance
Uganvanava: , Uganvanava	Teach
Bonava: , Bonava	Drink
A:dharaya karanava: , A:daraya karanava	Love
A:sa karanava: , A:sa karanava	Like
So:dhanava: , So:dhanava	Wash
Soyanava: , Soyanava	Look for/Search
Gahanava: , Gahanava	Hit
Naegitinava: , Naegitinava	Stand up, Wake up
Nidhiyanava: , Nidhiyanava *Nidha:gannava: , Nidha: gannava*	Sleep
Navanava: , Navanava	Fold
Hadhanava: , Hadhanava	Make
Kadanava: , Kadanava	Break
Igena gannava: , Igena gannava	Learn
Buranava: , Buranava	Bark

Sellam karanava: , Sellam karanava	Play
Sindhu kiyanava: , Sindhu kiyanava	Sing
Sinaha senava: , Sinaha senava	Laugh, Smile
Sithanava: , Sithanava	Think
Venas karanava: , Venas karanava *Venas venava:, Venas venava*	Change
Maninava: , Maninava	Measure
Pichchenava: , Pichchenava	Burn (as in "The candle burns.")
Puchchanava: , Puchchanava	Burn (as in " I burn the candle.")
visthara karanava: , visthara karanava	Describe
paehaedhili karanava: , paehaedhili karanava	Explain
makanava: , makanava	Erase
thi:ntha ga:nava: , thi:ntha ga:nava	Paint
aevidhinava: , aevidhinava	Walk
dhuvanava: , dhuvanava	Run
vikunanava: , vikunanava	Sell
a'ndanava: , a'ndanava	Cry
paninava: , paninava	Jump
peralanava: , peralanava	Turn (as in "turn a page")
haerenava: , haerenava	Turn (as in "I turned left)

Fundamental Sentence Pattern

Constructing a Sinhala sentence is very easy.

There is no difference between active and passive voice in spoken Sinhala.

You use the same sentence pattern for both active and passive voices in English. You do not vary the verb to agree with the subject (doesn't matter gender; doesn't matter singular/plural). Here is the general sentence pattern.

Doer + Object + Verb

The doer is the agent, the noun that does the verb. You already know what object and verb mean. If you have learnt the verbs and nouns in the previous lists, then you will easily understand the following Sinhala sentences!

> **Amma: bath uyanava: .**
> (The mother cooks rice.)

> **Lamaya: potha kiyavanava: .**
> (The child reads the book.)

Now, you can omit either or both doer and object. Usually you cannot omit the verb. If it is a sentence, there has to be some action (verb).

> **Amma: uyanava: .**
> (The mother cooks.)

> **Lamaya: kiyavanava: .**
> (The child reads.)

In above two immediate sentences, as you can see, we do not see objects. Likewise, we can omit the agents instead of the objects as follows.

Bath uyanava: .
(Rice is cooked.)

Potha liyanava: .
(The book is read.)

When the agent/doer is missing, you have to use passive voice in English. However, in Sinhala it is still the same sentence pattern – **no difference between active and passive voices structurally.**

You may even omit both the agent and the object as follows too. I do not know how to write it in English without both of them. Therefore, I have used a trick when giving the English meaning using "somebody" and "something". Here, the context will give you the missing words.

Uyanava: .
(*'somebody'* cooks *'something'*.).

Liyanava: .
(*'somebody'* reads *'something'*.)

You know when expressing an idea (or constructing a sentence) **in English**, there are two levels.

First level is just using the tenses (simple, continuous, perfect, and perfect continuous). You have three times of them too – past, present, and future.

The second level is formed on top of the first level. Here helping verbs like can, could, must, need are used. Generally, these two levels will enable you to express most if not all ideas.

In Sinhala too, you can find and follow this same method to grasp the grammar productively. In Sinhala, you have three tenses only.

Therefore, what we have already learned is both simple and continuous tense (in present time). Sinhala verbs (as listed above) like *karanava:* , *balanava:* , *natanava:* are automatically both simple tense and continuous tense.

Actually, for both simple and continuous tenses in English, there is only one verb form in Sinhala.

The continuous tense in English is used when you want to say something or some action that is happening at a particular moment. You use simple tense to say something that happens "*not* at a particular moment", but that happens everyday, regularly, naturally, customarily, etc. In Sinhala, this distinction is not there.

Amma: bath uyanava:
= the mother cooks rice.
= the mother is cooking rice.

Bath uyanava:
= rice is cooked.
= rice is being cooked.

Uyanava:
= "someone" cooks "something".
= "someone" is cooking "something".

As you can see,

the present time verbs having both continuous tense and simple tense meaning end with "-nava:"

Now construct some sentences using the verbs and nouns given in the above lists.

Following are some Sinhala sentences constructed according to the rules and practices mentioned above.

Ayya: potha kiyavanava:
(The elder brother reads the book.   Or
The elder brother is reading the book.)

Malli pa:n kanava:
(The younger brother eats bread.   Or
The younger brother is eating bread.)

Teacher uganvanava:
(The female teacher teaches.   Or
The female teacher is teaching.)

In Sinhala language, as in many other languages, you can find so many English words being used just as normal Sinhala words (as substitutes). Not only that, if you probably used the proper Sinhala word instead of the English substitute word, the native listeners would have even laughed at you. For example, the Sinhala word for the teacher is *"guruthumi:"* (feminine), and if you used *"guruthumi:"*instead of "teacher", natives would definitely laugh at you. Well, I do not know if laughing or scorning is right or wrong when a native uses a native word, but it would happen.

Some English words that you can use just as Sinhala words
(with the same original English meaning) are listed below.

bus	van	car	bicycle
motor cycle	seat	TV	radio
telephone	phone	hose	bag
driver	plane	helicopter	shirt
camera	toilet	bucket	computer
basket	hall	keyboard	printer
wire	cable	bulb	purse
switch (noun)	collar	shampoo	machine
antenna	accident	handle (noun)	sofa
photo	butter	cake	office
factory	motor	battery	charger
restaurant	cream	yogurt	engine
t-shirt	banner	garage	concrete
label	doctor	nurse	sticker
bra	rubber	bakery	ticket
rest house	ambulance	salon	poster
key tag	car park	handbag	pharmacy
park	parcel	cellphone	bill
mobile phone	smart phone	bed sheet	party
clip (noun)	pin (noun)	blade	fridge
CD	DVD	nut	job
helmet	petrol	diesel	jet
fan	horn	tyre	roundabout
traffic	lace	wifi	bluetooth
whiteboard	duster	chalk	badge
video camera	recorder	bat (that you use in sports)	
laptop		tie (that you wear)	
transformer (electric)		bus halt/ bus stand	
call (telephone call)		form (that you fill in)	
teacher (but only feminine, that is "female teacher)			

The above list can be much longer than that. However, there are some English words being used as much as the Sinhala words. One may use a Sinhala word; another may use an English word. Some such words along with the Sinhala word are:

room / ka:maraya	bathroom / na:na ka:maraya
pantry / kussiya	garden / vaththa
glass / vi:dhuruva	cap / thoppiya
cup / ko:ppaya	pocket / sa:kkuva
button / both thama	class / panthiya
market / pola	bank / baenkuva
clerk / lipikaru	book shop / poth sa:ppuva
shop / sa:ppuva	lawyer / ni:thi'gnaya
engineer / injine:ruva:	girl / gaehaenu lamaya:
boy / pirimi lamaya:	girlfriend / pemvathiya
boyfriend / pemvatha:	uncle / ma:ma:
aunty / naendha:	board / lae:lla
tea / the:	training / puhunuva
taste (noun) / rasa	powder / kudu
tattoo / pachchaya	diary / dhina potha
time / vela:va	place / thaena
drama / na:tya	hotel / ho:talaya
exam / viba:gaya	maths / ganithaya
science / vidhya:va	music / sangi:thaya
song / sindhuva	beach / verala
team / kanda:yama	filter (filtering device) / peranaya
film / chithrapatiya	watch (wrist watch) / oralo:suva
line / ira	exercise (for fit) / vya:ya:maya
belt / patiya	train (vehicle) / ko:chchiya
eraser / makanaya	blackboard / kalu lae:lla

I will show how to use English words in Sinhala sentences later. Depending on the context, most of the English words are "*Sinhalized*" (that is, made kind of compatible with Sinhala pronunciation pattern) with a few tricks that I will explain later.

Derived Sentence Patterns

Now that we know how to construct some valid Sinhala sentences (in present time) in the affirmative/positive statement form, let us learn how to modify the sentence to form five other variants of it. Not only in this particular case, but also in all other sentence patterns you can form these five variants:

1. Negative statement
2. Affirmative question
3. Negative question
4. Affirmative tag question
5. Negative tag question

Affirmative Question

First, let us see how to form the affirmative question. It is very easy. You just put

"dha"

at the end of the verb of the usual affirmative sentence.

Amma: bath uyanava: → **Amma: bath uyanava:dha?**
(Does the mother cook rice?
Is the mother cooking rice?)

Bath uyanava: → **Bath uyanava:dha?**
(Is rice cooked?
Is rice being cooked?)

Amma: uyanava: → **Amma: uyanava:dha?**
(Does the mother cook?
Is the mother cooking?)

Uyanava: → **Uyanava:dha?**
(Does "someone" cook "something"?
Is "someone" cooking "something"?)

Requests

This positive question form is also used to make a **request** (requesting somebody in front of you to do something) in Sinhala. You may also put "*karuna:karala*" (meaning "please"), or "*please*" itself at the beginning or the end of the sentence.

> **Oya: potha denava:dha?**
> (Can/Will you give the book?)
>
> **Karuna:karala e:ka kiyanavadha?**
> (Can/Could you please tell it?)
>
> **Pae:na denava:dha please?**
> (Can I have the pen please?)

Negative Statement

How to construct the negative statement? First, remember that you must use the word

"naehae"

which is equivalent to English "not". You put this word after the verb. In addition, you slightly modify the last few letters (last syllable) of the verb as follows (actually, it has a clear pattern). The verb ending "nava:" is modified to "**nne**" or "**nne:**".

"...nava:" → "...nne"

Amma: bath uyanava: → **Amma: bath <u>uyanne naehae</u>.**

(The mother does not cook rice.
The mother is not cooking rice.)

Bath uyanava: → **Bath uyanne naehae.**
(Rice is not cooked.
Rice is not being cooked.)

Amma: uyanava: → **Amma: uyanne naehae.**
(The mother does not cook.
The mother is not cooking.)

Uyanava: → **Uyanne naehae.**
("Someone" does not cook "something"
"Someone" is not cooking "something")

Negative Question

Ok. Now let us see how to make the negative question. Actually, it is the combination of above two techniques. You first make the negative statement, and then put "dha" at the end of "*naehae*"; so it becomes like "*naehaedha*". And very often, naehaedha is again changed to

"naedhdha"

(So it can be easily pronounced; nothing else).

From this moment on, I will not be writing all English forms of the same sentence structure as I have been doing. Instead, I would cite the longest sentence structure (with the doer, object, and verb).

Amma: bath uyanava: → **Amma: bath uyanne naedhdha?**

(Does the mother not cook rice?
Is the mother not cooking rice?)

Ayya: potha liyanava: → **Ayya: potha liyanne naedhdha?**
(Does the elder brother not write the book?
Is the elder brother not writing the book?)

Tag Questions

Last, let us learn how to make the two tag questions. Unlike in English, it is very very easy to construct them. You just use the tag

"ne:dha".

To make the affirmative tag question, you put it just after the verb.

And to make the negative tag question, you put it just after "naehae" of the normal negative statement; that is to, put

"naehae ne:dha"

at the end of the sentence.

Amma: bath uyanava: → **Amma: bath uyanava: ne:dha?**
(The mother cooks rice. Doesn't she?
The mother is cooking rice. Isn't she?)

Amma: bath uyanava: → **Amma: bath uyanne naehae ne:dha?**
(The mother doesn't cook rice. Does she?

The mother is not cooking rice. Is she?)

You can easily make all types (6) of sentence variations/forms of the same sentence as the following example shows. Using the verbs and nouns given in the first lesson, you should practice now constructing many examples. In the future lessons, you will learn more tenses and with them too, you can have these variations/forms.

Lamaya: potha kiyavanava: .
(The child is reading the book.
The child reads the book.)

Lamaya: potha kiyavanne naehae.
(The child is not reading the book.
The child does not read the book.)

Lamaya: potha kiyavanava:dha?
(Is the child reading the book?
Does the child read the book?)

Lamaya: potha kiyavanne naedhdha?
(Is the child not reading the book?
Does the child not read the book?)

Lamaya: potha kiyavanava: ne:dha?
(The child is reading the book. Isn't he?
The child reads the book. Doesn't he?)

Lamaya: potha kiyavanne naehae ne:dha?
(The child is not reading the book. Is he?
The child does not read the book. Does he?)

Sinhala Pronouns

As in other languages, the spoken Sinhala also has the following pronouns. The verb does not change depending on the pronoun.

Singular	Plural
Mama, Man (I)	**Api** (We)
Eya: (He or She)	**E:gollo** , **E:gollan** (They)
U: (It – animal)	**Un** (They – animals)
E:ka (It – thing)	**E:va**: (They – things)
Araka (That)	**Arava:** (Those)
Me:ka (This)	**Me:va:** (These)
O:na kenek (Anyone)	**Haemo:ma** (Everybody)
Kenek (Someone)	**Samaharu** , **Samaharun** (Some – about people)
Yamak (Something)	**Siyalla** (All – about things)
Oya: (You)	**O:gollo** , **O:gollan** (You)
Oba (You – honorary)	**Obala:** (You – honorary)

Mama yanava: .
(I am going.
I go.)

Api yanava: .
(We are going.
We go.)

Eya: yanava: .
(She/He is going.
He/She goes.)

O:gollo yanava: .
(You are going.
You go.)

U: kanne naehae.
(It is not eating.
It does not eat.)

Un kanne naehae.
(They are not eating.
They do not eat.)

Mama pa:n kanne naehae.
(I am not eating bread.
I do not eat bread.)

Oya: yanava:dha?
(Are you going?
Do you go?)

Egollo yanava:dha?
(Are they going?
Do they go?)

Forming WH-questions in Sinhala

Earlier, we learnt how to make "Yes/No" questions, and the two tag questions. Now let us learn how to make "**Wh-**" questions. Just as in English, Sinhala too has the few keywords similar to the English "Wh-" words as follows.

Mokakdha – what

Ko:kadha – which

Aeyi – why

Kohomadha – how

Kohe:dha – where

Kavudha – who

Ka:vadha – whom

Ki:yatadha – at what time (when)

Kavadhdha / **Kavadhadha** – at which day/date (when)

You know the usual sentence order (doer + object + verb). You can put one of above question words

- before the doer or
- after the doer (and before the object) or
- before the verb (and after the doer) or
- after the verb

Yes, all these three forms are same and popular equally. Just placing the question word is not enough. You have to modify the ending of the verb from "-nava:" to "-nne" (You learnt this modification earlier too). Let us take an example.

Eya: potha kiyavanava:

Kohomadha eya: potha kiyavanne?
Eya: kohomadha potha kiyavanne?
Eya: potha kohomadha kiyavanne?
Eya: potha kiyavanne kohomadha?
(How is he reading the book?
How does he read the book?)

Kohe:dha eya: potha kiyavanne?
Eya: kohe:dha potha kiyavanne?
Eya: potha kohe:dha kiyavanne?
Eya: potha kiyavanne kohe:dha?
(Where is he reading the book?
Where does he read the book?)

Aeyi eya: potha kiyavanne?
Eya: aeyi potha kiyavanne?
Eya: potha aeyi kiyavanne?
Eya: potha kiyavanne aeyi?
(Why is he reading the book?
Why does he read the book?)

Ki:yatadha eya: potha kiyavanne?
Eya: ki:yatadha potha kiyavanne?
Eya: potha ki:yatadha kiyavanne?
Eya: potha kiyavanne ki:yatadha?
(When is he reading the book?
When does he read the book?)

Let us see a few more questions. As you know now, both the continuous and simple tense meanings are there in this single Sinhala sentence pattern. Therefore, I will not write both tenses as the meaning of a Sinhala sentence, and instead I will be only citing either tense for simplicity from this moment on.

Mokakdha oya: karanne?
Oya: mokakdha karanne?
Oya: karanne mokakdha?
(What are you doing?)

Ko:kadha oya: kanne?
Oya: ko:kadha kanne?
Oya: kanne ko:kadha?
(Which are you eating?)

Ka:vadha mama ganne?
Mama ka:vadha ganne?
Mama ganne ka:vadha?
(Whom am I taking?)

Kavudha bath kanne?
Bath kavudha kanne?
Bath kanne kavudha?
(Who is eating rice?)

Kavudha oya:?
Oya: kavudha?
(Who are you?)

Kavudha eya:?
Eya: kavudha?
(Who is he/she?)

You know there is no difference between active voice sentence structure and passive voice sentence structure in Sinhala. Remembering the learned points, read and understand the following sentences.

Aeyi potha kiyavanne?
Potha aeyi kiyavanne?
Potha kiyavanne aeyi?
(Why is the book read?)

Kohe:dha bath uyanne?
Bath kohe:dha uyanne?
Bath uyanne kohe:dha?
(Where is rice cooked?)

Kavadhadha e:ka karanne?
E:ka kavadhadha karanne?
E:ka karanne kavadhdha?
(When is it done?)

Kohomadha e:ka karanne?
E:ka kohomadha karanne?
E:ka karanne kohomadha?
(How is it done?)

Mokakdha sidhdha venne?
Sidhdha venne mokakdha?
(What happens?)

Ka:vadha maranne?
Maranne ka:vadha?
(Who is killed?)

Adjectives and Adverbs

Let us now learn about adjectives and adverbs in Sinhala. First, learn the following adjectives.

Adjective	Meaning
Lassana	Beautiful
Kaetha	Ugly
Usa	Tall, High
Miti, Kota	Short
Mahatha	Fat
Hi:ni, Kettu	Thin, Slim
Loku	Big
Podi	Small
Bara	Heavy
Saehaellu	Light
Pohosath	Rich
Duppath	Poor
Ganan	Expensive
La:ba	Cheap
Ho'ndha	Good
Naraka	Bad
Rasa	Tasty, Sweet
Thiththa	Bitter
Eaththa	True

Boru	False
Pissu	Mad
Saera	Strict, Hot (like chili)
Viyali, Ve:lichcha	Dry
Theth, Thetha	Wet
Ga'ndha	Smelly
Suva'ndha	Fragrant
Vatina:	Valuable
Pirisi'ndhu	Clean
Vaedhagath	Important
Ahinsaka	Innocent
Napuru	Cruel
Ugath	Learned
Mo:da	Foolish
Dhaksha	Clever, Smart
Nithara	Frequent

Colors in Sinhala

Following is the list of colors. In Sinhala, each color name is both an adjective and a noun, similar to the English practice.

However, you can put the word "***pa:ta***" (*pa:ta* means "color") after the color name to make it an explicit noun. For example, "***sudu pa:ta***" means the "**red color**".

You can put *"la:"* in front of a color name to mean "**light** color", and *"thadha"* to mean "**dark** color". For example, *"la: rathu"* means "**light red**", and *"thadha rathu"* means "**dark red**".

Color	Meaning
Sudhu	White
Kalu	Black
Rathu	Red
Nil	Blue
Kola	Green
Kaha	Yellow
Dham	Purple
Alu	Grey
Thae'nbili	Orange
Dhu'nburu	Brown
Ran, Raththaran	Gold
Ridi:	Silver
Ro:sa	Pink

As you do in English, you

put an adjective in front of a noun.

That's it. You can put any number of consecutive adjectives as many as you want.

Lassana lamaya: loku potha kiyavanava: .
(The **beautiful** child is reading the **big** book.)

Ho'ndha **amma: bath uyanava: .**
(The **good** mother is cooking rice.)

Usa kettu **lamaya: duvanava: .**
(The **tall thin** child is running.)

Duppath **tha:ththa:** *rathu* **potha gannava: .**
(The **poor** father is taking/buying the **red** book.)

Mama *la: kola* **gaha kapanava: .**
(I am cutting the **light green** tree.)

How to form Sinhala adverbs from adjectives

Just as an adjective describes a noun, an adverb describes a verb.
In Sinhala too (as in English), you make most of the adverbs out
of adjectives. In English you put the suffix "-ly" at the end of the
adjective to form the relevant adverb. In Sinhala, in fact there
are about four suffixes that you can use to make the adverb:

"-ta"   "-in"   "-en"   "-va"

However, there is no set of rules to determine the correct suffix.

Lassana → Lassana**ta** (beautifully)

Kaetha → Kaetha**ta** (ugly)

Ho'ndha → Ho'ndha**ta** (well)
              → Ho'ndh**in** (well)

Pirisidhu → Pirisidhu**va** (cleanly)

Naraka → Narak**en** (badly)
    → Narak**in** (badly)
    → Narak**ata** (badly)

Actually, there is some complexity in making adverbs (this same complexity exists in English too). Sometimes the ending syllable of the adjective is modified; that is, one or more ending letters may be deleted/elided, and/or one or more letters may be brought in from outside.

However, when you get familiar with the words and sounds, and when you learn more and more words, you will find that there are some intuitive reasons for letters being deleted and brought from outside. For example,

Naraka + in → Narakin (the ending "a" is deleted)

Loku + ta → Lokuvata ("va" is brought in from outside)

Following is a list of some irregular adverbs (those which are not made out of adjectives). As you are well aware, there are tons of adverbs of this nature in English too.

Adverb	Meaning
Adha	Today
I:ye	Yesterday
Heta	Tomorrow
Dhaen	Now
Passe	Later
Pere:dha:	The day before yesterday
Anidhdha:	The day after tomorrow

La'ngadhi	Lately, soon
Itha:	Very, Too, So
Ithin	So (as in "so, what happened?")
I:ta passe	After that
E:nisa:, Ema nisa:	Therefore
Eheth, E: una:ta	However
E:ka neme:	By the way
Mona: unath, Mokak unath	Anyway
E: vidiyata, Ehema	Like that
Me: vidiyata, Mehema	Like this
A:yeth	Again
Ovu	Yes
Naehae	No
Issara, E: davasvala	Earlier, Those days
Me: davasvala	These days
Kohomahari	Somehow or other

Usually the adverb is put in front of the verb

(just as you put the adjective in front of the noun). And, you can put as many adverbs as you want.

Eya: *lassanata* **liyanava:**
(He is writing beautifully.)

Amma: *ho'ndhata* **bath uyanava:**
(The mother is cooking rice well.)

Lamaya: *ho'ndhata lassanata* **liyanava:**
(The child writes well and beautifully.)

Api haemadha:ma sathutin TV balanava: .
(We watch TV happily everyday.)

Actually, you may put the adverb at the beginning, at the end, or after the verb too.

Eya: liyanava: *lassanata.*
(He is writing beautifully.)

Haemadha:ma sathutin api TV balanava: .
(We watch TV happily everyday.)

Future Tenses in Sinhala

Now let us learn how to express something that is going to happen in the future (that is, construction of the future tense sentences). There are mainly three ways. We will consider all forms (like negative statement, questions, etc) of the same sentence.

1ˢᵗ method

There is nothing to learn anew in the first method. Actually, you can use the same present time sentence you have been learning so far here. Usually you use an *adverb* (like tomorrow) that denotes future with that too (it is not required though).

> **Stephanie *heta* e:ka kiyanava: .**
> (Stephanie will tell it tomorrow.)

> **Api *anidhdha:* yanava: .**
> (We will go day after tomorrow.)

> **Egollo e:ka karanava: .**
> (They will do it.)

The negative statement form is just the same negative statement that you have already learned.

> Mama heta yanava: . → **Mama heta yanne naehae.**
> (I will not go tomorrow.)

> Sara anidhdha: enava: . → **Sara anidhdha: enne naehae.**
> (Sara will not come day after tomorrow.)

Not only the negative statement, the other forms (positive question, negative question, etc) are the same as what you had learnt before.

Mama heta yanava:dha?
(Will I go tomorrow?)

Sara anidhdha: enava:dha?
(Will Sara come day after tomorrow?)

Mama heta yanne nadhdha?
(Will I not go tomorrow?)

Sara anidhdha: enne nadhdha?
(Will Sara not come day after tomorrow?)

Mama heta yanava: ne:dha?
(I will go tomorrow. Won't I?)

Sara anidhdha: enava: ne:dha?
(Sara will come day after tomorrow. Won't she?)

Mama heta yanne naehae ne:dha?
(I will not go tomorrow. Will I?)

Sara anidhdha: enne naehae ne:dha?
(Sara will not come day after tomorrow. Will she?)

2ⁿᵈ method

There is another popular way of expressing something in future (the second method). In that sentence pattern, you just change the ending of "-nava:" verb. To construct this future tense verb, you first remove the "-nava:" part, and then you append **"-a:vi"**.

…nava: → …a:vi

*Balanava: → Bala~nava:~ + a:vi → **Bala:vi** (will look)*

*Karanava: → Karara~nava:~ + a:vi → **Kara:vi** (will do)*

Now you can make future tense sentences as follows.

Shane ya:vi.
(Shane will go.)

Ayda bath uya:vi.
(Ayda will cook rice.)

Gasa kapa:vi.
(The tree will be cut.)

Amma: heta bath uya:vi.
(The mother will cook rice tomorrow.)

The negative statement of this second kind of future tense
pattern is as same as the normal negative statement you already
know.

Shane yanne naehae.
(Shane will not go.)

(Remember this same sentence has the meaning of
"*Shane does not go*" and "*Shane is not going*"; take the
correct meaning based on the context)

Ayda bath uyanne naehae.
(Ayda will not cook rice.)
(Also, "*Ayda does not cook rice*" and "*Ayda is not
cooking rice*")

To form the positive question, you just add "-**dha**" at the end of
the verb of the positive statement as follows.

Shane ya:vidha?
(Will Shane go?)

Ayda bath uya:vidha?
(Will Ayda cook rice?)

The negative question is formed like this. First assume that "-nava:" verb form is there; now remove "va:" from that verb. After that, you put "**ekak naehae**" at the end.

...nava: → ...na ekak naehae

Shane ya:vi. → (Shane yana~~va:~~ + ekak naehae) → **Shane yana ekak naehae.**
(Shane will not go.)

Ayda bath uya:vi. → (Ayda bath uyana~~va:~~ + ekak naehae) → **Ayda bath uyana ekak naehae.**
(Ayda will not cook rice.)

Oya: e:ka kiyana ekak naehae.
(You will not tell it.)

Indefinite Future with I and We

However, the above form of future tense is not used with a subject of "I" or "We" (first person pronouns). If you use this form of verb with "I" or "We", it would be a future time sentence of course, but additionally that sentence will mean an indefinite expression (uncertain whether or not the action will be done). In short, such a sentence is expressed in English with the helping verbs of "may, might".

Man ya:vi.
(I may go. / I will probably go.)

Api e:ka kara:vi.
(We may do it. / We will probably do it.)

Indefinite Future

Surprisingly, if you want to express an indefinite future tense (just as discussed in the previous paragraph) with any subject (in addition to I and We), we use this same sentence. Therefore, this sentence pattern has two meanings with any noun/subject – one is "normal future tense", and the other is "indefinite future tense".

Eya: ya:vi.
(He will probably go. / He may go.)

Natalie e:vi.
(Natalie may come. / Natalie will probably come.)

Oya: e:ka kiya:vi.
(You may tell it. / You will probably tell it.)

Shane ya:vidha?
(May Shane go?)

Ayda bath uya:vidha?
(May Ayda cook rice?)

Shane yana ekak naehae.
(Shane may not go.)

Ayda bath uyana ekak naehae.
(Ayda may not cook rice.)

3ʳᵈ method

The third method is exclusive for the subject of "I" or "We" (first person pronouns). It is similar to English "shall" sentences. Here, the "-nava:" ending of the verb is changed to "**-nnam**".

…nava: → …nnam

Mama yanava: . → **Mama yannam.**
(I shall go.)

Api e:ka kohomahari karannam.
(We shall do it somehow or other.)

Mama potha liyannam.
(I shall write the book.)

The negative statement of this type of sentence is as same as normal negative statement.

Mama yanne naehae.
(I shall not go.)

Api e:ka karanne naehae.
(We shall not do it.)

Mama potha liyanne naehae.
(I will not write the book)

Requests Revisited…

The positive question form is used here. You remove "m" from the verb (let us call this verb participle "**nna verb**" from this moment on), and append "dha". Actually, this is how we make request in Sinhala too.

…nnam ➔ …nnadha?

Karannam → Karanna̶m̶ + dha = ***karannadha***

Mama yannadha?
(Shall/May I go?)

Api e:ka karannadha?
(Shall/May we do it?)

Mama TV balannadha?
(Shall/May I watch TV?)

Last, let us make the negative request. First remove "m" from the verb like we did earlier (that is, make the "nna verb"), and put "***epa:dha***" after that.

…nnam ➔ …nna epa:dha?

Karannam → Karanna̶m̶ epa:dha = ***karanna epa:dha***

Mama yanna epa:dha?
(Shall/May I not go?)

Api e:ka karanna epa:dha?
(Shall/May we not do it?)

Mama TV bala nna epa:dha?
(Shall/May I not watch TV?)

Be going to ...

There is another way to make a future tense sentence. It is
similar to "**be going to**" sentence pattern in English. Here, we
use the "nna verb" and after that we put "*yanne*" / "*yanne:*" or
"*yanava:*" / "*yanava*" or "*inne:*" / "*inne*".

$$...nnam \rightarrow ...nna \text{ yanne:}$$
$$...nnam \rightarrow ...nna \text{ inne:}$$

Mama potha kiyavanna yanne/yanava:/inne .
(I am going to read the book.)

Eya: nidiyanna yanava:/yanne/inne.
(She/He is going to sleep.)

The negative forms and question forms of this type of sentence
can be constructed with the knowledge you have obtained so far
by following the lessons.

Mama potha kiyavanna yanne naehae.
(I am not going to read the book.)

Mama potha kiyavannadha yanne?
(Am I going to read the book?)

To form the negative form, there is another way. Here, you put
"*neme:*" or "*ne mei*" just before the "*inne*" or "*yanne*".

Mama gedhara yanna neme: inne.
(I am not going to go home.)

Shelly e:ka kiyanna neme: yanne: .
(Shelly is not going to tell it.)

To make the negative question, you have to use "*neme:dha*" or "*nemeidha*".

Mama gedhara yanna neme:dha inne?
(Am I not going to go home?)

Shelly e:ka kiyanna neme:dha yanne?
(Is Shelly not going to tell it?)

This pattern also has the English meaning of "**be planning to**" or "**be about to**". They also give kind of future meaning.

Mama potha kiyavanna inne/innava: .
(I am planning to read the book. / I am about to read the book.)

Eya: nidyanna inne/innava: .
(He/She is planning to sleep.)

Commands in Sinhala

Let us make commands in Sinhala now. It is very easy. Always the command is directed to the person in your presence (that is, "**you**"). It is the same as in English. Follow the normal Sinhala sentence order. Here, the doer is "*oya:*" (singular) or "*o:gollo/o:gollan, oya:la:*" (plural) subject. You can omit it if you like (as in English).

There is a small change in the verb ending; you just put the "nna verb" instead of the normal "-nava: verb" form.

…nava: → …nna

Oya: yanna.
(You go.)

Yanna.
(Go.)

Oya: bath ho'ndhin kanna.
(You eat rice well.)

Bath kanna.
(Eat rice.)

Ogollo loku potha kiyavanna.
(You (plural) read the big book.)

Potha kiyavanna.
(Read the book.)

To give a command not to do something, you just put "**epa**:" after verb, or before the subject (if existing), or after the subject (whether or not it exists).

...nava: → ...nna epa:

Oya: yanna epa: .
Epa: oya: yanna.
Oya: epa: yanna.
(You don't go.)

Yanna epa: .
Epa: yanna.
(Don't go.)

Oya: bath kanna epa: .
Epa: oya: bath kanna.
Oya epa: bath kanna.
(You don't eat rice.)

Bath kanna epa: .
Epa: bath kanna.
(Don't eat rice.)

Ogollan potha kiyavanna epa: .
Epa: ogollan potha kiyavanna.
Ogollan epa: potha kiyavanna.
(You don't read the book.)

Potha kiyavanna epa: .
Epa: potha kiyavanna.
(Don't read the book.)

If you want to make the command more polite, you can put
"*karuna:karala*" (please) at the beginning or the end of the
command.

> **Karuna:karala oya: yanna.**
> **Oya: yanna karuna:karala.**
> (You go please.)
>
> **Karuna:karala yanna**
> **Yanna karuna:karala.**
> (Go please.)
>
> **Karuna:karala oya: yanna epa: . / Oya: yanna epa:**
> **karuna:karala.**
> **Karuna:karala epa: oya: yanna. / Epa: oya: yanna**
> **karuna:karala.**
> **Karuna:karala oya: epa: yanna. / Oya: epa: yanna**
> **karuna:karala.**
> (You don't go please.)
>
> **Karuna:karala yanna epa: . / Yanna epa:**
> **karuna:karala.**
> **Karuna:karala epa: yanna. / Epa: yanna**
> **karuna:karala.**
> (Don't go please.)

If you like, you can substitute "*please*" for "karuna:karala" too.
For example,

> **Please oya: yanna. / Oya: yanna please.**
> (Please go.)
>
> **Please yanna epa: . / Yanna epa: please.**
> (Please don't go.)

Plea

You can make the command milder. And it probably can be considered as a plea now (instead of a command). For that, you append "**-ko:**" or "**-ko**" to the "nna verb". You may include "*please*" or "*karuna:karala*" to make it "much milder". There is no negative form of this.

…nava: → …nnako:

Oya: yannako.
Yannako oya:
Yannako.
(Go. Will you?)

Oya: gedhara yannako: .
Gedhara yannako oya.
Gedhara yannako.
(You go home. Will you?)

Strong or Friendly Commands

You can also make the command stronger/stringent. You specially use this form of command when you are mad at somebody (or scolding somebody or in a quarrel, etc). You never use this form of command at your parents, older relatives, teachers, honorable people, etc. It is harsh.

To make this harsh command, you put a verb made as follows (you remove the "nava:" from the "nava: verb" form, and append "**pan**" to it). No negative form of this exists.

…nava: → …pan

*Karanava: → Kara̶n̶a̶v̶a̶: + pan = **Karapan***

Potha liyapan.
(Read the book.)

Gedhara palayan.
(Go home.)

Surprisingly, this same command form is used <u>among friends</u> too. Then it has no harsh meaning, but instead it gets a friendly meaning. In this situation, you may add *"please"* or *"karuna:karala"* to this command. Never use this type of sentence to address adults.

Karuna:karala attha kiyapan.
(Tell the truth please.)

Singular and Plural Nouns

So far, in the lessons, I made sure not to use plural nouns (except plural forms of pronouns). In Sinhala, nouns are somewhat complicated than in English. In English, almost all nouns are automatically singular, and you make plural of them by appending "s" or "es" at the end of the noun.

However, in Sinhala both the singular and plural nouns are formed from "noun stems/roots". Learning about noun roots, and deriving various forms out of them is deep and complicated, and even the native Sinhala speaker does not know much about it. Therefore, we will keep that linguistically correct way of learning about nouns aside. Let us take a different and easy approach.

I suggest you to study both singular and plural forms when you study Sinhala words in the initial stage of learning. At once, it would seem like a daunting task, but it is not. There is an intuitive relationship between the singular and plural forms of a noun, and you will grasp it gradually.

There are a set of grammatical rules on how to relate the two forms (of noun) to each other. However, I feel it is not required or important to know all these rules; it will not do any good. I will list some nouns in both forms.

Singular	Plural
Mala (the flower)	**Mal** (flowers)
Gala (the stone)	**Gal** (stones)
Potha (the book)	**Poth** (books)
Pae:na (the pen)	**Pae:n** (pens)

Gasa (the tree)	**Gas** (trees)
Kalisama (the pair of trousers)	**Kalisam** (pairs of trousers)
Datha (the tooth)	**Dath** (teeth)
Aesa (the eye)	**Aes** (eyes)
Kana (the ear)	**Kan** (ears)
Atha (the hand)	**Ath** (hands)
Kakula (the leg)	**Kakul** (legs)
Paensala (the pencil)	**Paensal** (pencils)
Mula (the root)	**Mul** (roots)
Gama (the village)	**Gam, Gamaval** (villages)
Balla: (the dog)	**Ballo: / Ballan** (dogs)
Pu:sa: (the cat)	**Pu:so: / Pu:san** (cats)
Mi:ya: (the rat)	**Mi:yo: / Mi:yan** (rats)
Ka:kka: (the crow)	**Ka:kko: / Ka:kkan** (crows)
Kurulla: (the bird)	**Kurullo: / Kurullan** (birds)
Kotiya: (the tiger)	**Kotiyo: / Kotiyan** (tigers)
Samanalaya: (the butterfly)	**Samanalayo: / Samanalayan** (butterflies)
Maessa: (the fly)	**Maesso: / Maessan** (flies)
Miniha: , Minisa: (the man)	**Minissu / Minisun** (men)
Gaehaeniya, Gaehaeni (the woman)	**Gaehaenu / Gaehaenun** (women)
Satha: (the animal)	**Saththu / Sathun** (animals)
Aemathivaraya: (the minister)	**Aemathivaru / Aeathivarun** (ministers)

Guruvaraya: (the male teacher)	**Guruvaru / Guruvarun** (teachers)
Nagaraya (the city)	**Nagara / Nagaraval** (cities)
Pihiya (the knife)	**Pihi** (knives)
Kadaya (the shop)	**Kada** (shops)
Putuva (the chair)	**Putu** (chairs)
Me:saya (the table)	**Me:sa** (tables)
Ka:maraya (the room)	**Ka:mara** (rooms)
Pa:ra (the road)	**Pa:raval** (roads)
Rata (the country)	**Rataval** (countries)
Nahaya (the nose)	**Nahayaval** (noses)
Bada (the stomach/belly)	**Badaval** (bellies)
Kata (the mouth)	**Kataval** (mouths)
Ge: / Geya (the house)	**Geval** (houses)
Dhora (the door)	**Dhoraval** (the doors)
Pola (the fair/market)	**Polaval** (fairs/markets)
Putha: (the son)	**Putha:la: / Puththu / Puthun** (sons)
Duva (the daughter)	**Duvala:** (daughters)
Amma: (the mother)	**Ammala:** (mothers)
Tha:ththa: (the father)	**Tha:ththala:** (fathers)
Si:ya: (the grandfather)	**Si:yala:** (grandfathers)
A:chchi (the grandmother)	**A:chchila:** (grandmothers)
Ayya: (the elder brother)	**Ayyala:** (elder brothers)

Akka: (the elder sister)	**Akkala:** (elder sisters)
Malli (the younger brother)	**Mallila:** (younger brothers)
Nangi (the younger sister)	**Nangila:** (younger sisters)
Ma:ma: (the uncle – a brother of mother or a husband of a father's sister or any elderly male person)	**Ma:mala:** (uncles)
Naenda: (the aunty – the wife a "ma:ma:")	**Naendala:** (aunties)
Ba:ppa: (the uncle – a younger brother of father or a husband of a mother's younger sister)	**Ba:ppala:** (uncles)
Punchi (the aunty – the wife of a "ba:ppa:"	**Punchila:** (aunties)
Mahappa: (the uncle – an elder brother of father or a husband of a mother's elder sister)	**Mahappala:** (uncles)
Loku amma: (the aunty – the wife of a "mahappa:"	**Loku ammala:** (aunties)
Muhuna (the face)	**Muhunu** (faces)
Oluva (the head)	**Olu / Oluvaval** (heads)
Bo:thalaya (the bottle)	**Bo:thal** (bottles)
Vaththa (the garden)	**Vathu, Vaththaval** (gardens)
Lamaya: (the child)	**Lamayi / Lamayin** (children)

Study and memorize the above nouns (both singular and plural forms). Then, you will see some patterns. The more nouns you learn, the clearer and easier the pattern will be. Trust me. Anyway, I very briefly point out the mostly used patterns.

1. The ending vowel in the singular noun is omitted. Sometimes nouns ending with "ya" or "wa" lose it too.

Mala, Gala, Mula, Pihiya, Putuva

2. "-val" is suffixed to the singular noun to make it plural. While doing so, some nouns (especially ones ending with "ya") lose the ending syllable.

Pa:ra, Bada, Nagaraya

3. The ending vowel of some nouns change to "o:" or "an" to make it plural.

Balla:, Pu:sa:, mi:ya:

4. All the nouns ending with "varaya:" are made plural by changing it to "varu" or "varun".

Guruvaraya:, Aemathivaraya:

5. "-la" is suffixed to make plural. While doing so, the stretched/long vowel sound at the end of the singular noun is made short too.

Ayya:, Nangi, Malli

Definite and Indefinite Nouns

In English, a noun can be either definite (with the article "the")
or indefinite (with the article "a/an" in the singular case or
without any article in the plural case).

Sinhala has this definite/indefinite distinction only in singular
nouns. In plural, the same plural noun form is used in either
definite or indefinite meaning.

Automatically the singular noun is definite. To make it indefinite
you append

> "**-ek**" (for masculine animate nouns) or
> "**-ak**" (for inanimate and feminine animate nouns)

to the singular noun. Just as English "a/an" has the meaning of
"one", Sinhala "-ek / -ak" has the same meaning.

> Lamaya: (the child) → **Lamayek** (a child)
>
> Miniha: (the man) → **Minihek** (a man)
>
> Gaehaeniya (the woman) → **Gaehaeniyak** (women)
>
> Mala (the flower) → **Malak** (a flower)
>
> Paena (the pen) → **Paenak** (a pen)

As you can see, the last syllable of some nouns is modified so
that the word is easily soundable / pronounceable (for example,
dropping the last vowel). Actually, to ease pronunciation, it is
done so in any language. It is a linguistic norm. When you get
familiar with the language, you will intuitively do it.

Note that in the spoken Sinhala, there is no clear difference in nominative case (when a noun is used as a subject) and objective case (when a noun is used as an object). Let us see some examples using definite and indefinite nouns.

Lamaya: pothak kiyavanava: .
(The child reads / is reading a book.)

Lamayek pothak kiyavanava: .
(A child reads / is reading a book.)

Lamaya: potha kiyavanava: .
(The child reads / is reading the book.)

Lamayek potha kiyavanava: .
(A child reads / is reading the book.)

Pothak kiyavanna.
(Read a book.)

Mama poth kiyavanava: .
(I read / am reading the books.
I read / am reading books.)

Geval so:danna.
(Wash the houses.
Wash houses.)

Mama yahaluvek ekka sellam karanava: .
(I play / am playing with a friend.)

Read the next lesson to know about the word "*ekka*" that you found in one example above, which is a preposition in Sinhala.

Prepositions

Now let us learn about **Sinhala prepositions** (like on, in, from, to, etc). Clearly, there are many Sinhala prepositions, some of which I list below. You must memorize these words first.

Preposition	Meaning
Uda, Matha	On
Gaena, Pili'nbadha	About (as in "information about you")
Yata, Yatin, Pahalin	under
Paeththen	beside
Udin, Ihalin	Above, Over
Issarahin , Idiriyen	In front of
Pitipassen, Pitupasin	Behind
Athara	Between, Among
Ekka, Sama'nga	With
Naethiva, Haera	Without, Except
Pamana, Vithara	About (as in "about 100 dollars")
Vate:ta	Around (as in "around the table")
Sa'ndhaha:	For
Venuven	On behalf of, For
Thulin	Through
Thek, Venakal, Thuru	Till/Until (a time), as far as (a place)
Pura: , Pura:vata	During
Pera, Issara	Before, Ago

Thula, Aethule: , -e:	In
Thulata, Aethulata	Into
Eliyata, Pitathata	Outside
Harahata	Across
Dhige:	Along
Osse:	Via, through
Visin, Magin	By
Vetha, Dhesa	At (as in "look at me")
La'nga, Asala	Near, At (as in "he is waiting at the gate")
Sita	From (a place), Since (a time)
-gen , -en/-in	From (a person or place)
-ge: , -e:	Of
Vaeni, Vage:	Like
Lesa, Vasayen	As
-ta	To
Vetha, Vethata	Towards

Like in English, the preposition does not change with respect to noun; but unlike in English, there are some differences when using Sinhala prepositions.

Sinhala prepositions are placed after the noun (but in English, it is put in front of a noun).

> **Me:saya uda** – *On the table*
> **Me:sayak uda** – *On a table*
> **Me:sa uda** – *On the tables / On tables*

Moreover, some of the prepositions are suffixed to the noun. In the above list, I have shown them clearly with a hyphen ("-en").

Sherin + -gen → **Sheringen** *(from Sherin)*

Anne + -ge → **Annege** *(of Anne)*

Gasa + -en → **Gasen** *(from the tree)*

Gasak + -in → **Gasakin** *(from a tree)*

Ahasa + -e: → **Ahase:** *(in the sky or of the sky)*

Atha + -e: → **Athe:** *(in the hand or of the hand)*

You know a preposition links a noun in a particular way to a sentence. You can put a preposition (with its attached noun) in the beginning, in the middle, or in the end of a sentence. The order of the prepositions is not important too.

Sherin ekka amma: yanava: .
Amma: Sherin ekka yanava: .
Amma: yanava: Sherin ekka.
(The mother goes / is going with Sherin.)

Sherin ekka amma: pa:ra dige: yanava: .
Pa:ra dige: Sherin ekka amma: yanava: .
Sherin ekka pa:ra dige: amma: yanava: .
Amma: yanava: Sherin ekka pa:ra dige: .
Amma: yanava: pa:ra dige: Sherin ekka.
(The mother goes / is going along the road with Sherin.)

Adoption of English Words in Sinhala

Earlier I told you that many English words are used in Sinhala. There are some implicit rules/norms when you use those English nouns, and there is a good underpinning for those rules. Here we are concerned about nouns only.

Almost all English nouns (and other words too) do not end with a vowel sound (that is, English words end with a consonant). However, most Sinhala words end with a vowel (that is, Sinhala words end with a vowel).

This is actually a very crucial thing because a person who is accustomed to speak/pronounce English may find difficult to pronounce/speak Sinhala, and vice versa.

Usually almost all Sinhala verbs (in whatever modified forms) end with a vowel sound. Almost all singular Sinhala nouns end with a vowel sound. Many plural Sinhala nouns also end with a vowel sound (and many end with consonant sound too). So do most of other types of words (like prepositions, adjectives).

Therefore, consonant-sounding singular English nouns are not used as it is. To make it more compatible with the usual Sinhala pronunciation, we put "**eka**" (to form the definite noun) or "**ekak**" (to form the indefinite noun) after the English noun.

> **Phone eka** *(the phone)*
> **Phone ekak** *(a phone)*
>
> **Bus eka** *(the bus)*
> **Bus ekak** *(a bus)*

Car eka (the car)
Car ekak (a car)

Note:

However, sometimes some English nouns are *treated* like normal Sinhala nouns; especially those nouns which end with a vowel sound. Only a few such nouns exist, so you do not have to worry much about them. One such example is "sofa".

So:fa:va (the sofa)
So:fa:vak (a sofa)
So:fa: (the sofas or sofas)

However, because the most of the plural Sinhala nouns have a consonant-sound at the end of the noun, you just use the singular English noun that ends with a consonant, as it is, in the plural meaning in Sinhala usage. You do not put "s" or "es" to make the English noun plural here. (Actually, it is not right to apply grammar of another language even if you may borrow words from it.)

Therefore, automatically almost all English nouns are considered plural within Sinhala (it is due to the fact that they end with a consonant sound).

Bus (the buses or buses)
Car (the cars or cars)
Phone (the phones or phones)

Now let us make some sentences with English nouns.

Shaun phone eka gannava: .
(Shaun takes the phone.)

Amma: car ekak elavanava: .
(The mother drives a car.)

Man car balanava: .
(I am seeing cars.)

In English, you connect a noun (or a noun clause) to the sentence with a preposition, and the preposition with the attached noun is usually placed after the verb. However, you know that it can be placed in other places, like at the beginning. You can add as many prepositions as you want. You can do the same in Sinhala, but the usual place to put a preposition and its attached noun is after the doer (before the object).

Mama gedharata yanava: .
Mama yanava: gedharata.
(I am going to the house.)

Mama gedharakata yanava: .
Mama yanava: gedharakata.
(I am going to a house.)

Eya: Paris sita enava: .
Eya: enava: Paris sita.
(He is coming from Paris.)

Akka: malli ekkapa:ra dhigegamata yanava: .
Akka: malli ekkapa:ra dhige yanava: gamata.
Akka: malli ekkagamata yanava: pa:ra dhige.
Akka: malli ekka yanava: pa:ra dhigegamata.

Akka: pa:ra dhigegamata yanava: malli ekka .
Akka: gamata yanava: malli ekka pa:ra dhige.
Akka: yanava: malli ekka pa:ra dhigegamata.
(The elder sister is going with the little brother along the road to the village.)

Kurulla: ahase: piya:'nbanava: .
Kurulla: piya:'nbanava: ahase: .
(The bird is flying in the sky.)

Kurulla: ahase: nidahase piya:'nbanava: .
(The bird is flying freely in the sky.)

Guruvaraya:gen ahanna.
Ahanna guruvaraya:gen.
(Ask from the teacher.)

Guruvarayekgen ahanna.
Ahanna guruvarayekgen.
(Ask from a teacher.)

Gasen Oxygen labenava: .
Oxygen gasen labenava: .
(Oxygen is obtained from the tree.)

Gasakin Oxygen labenava: .
Oxygen gasaki labenava: .
(Oxygen is obtained from a tree.)

Gasvalin Oxygen labenava: .
Oxygen gasvalin labenava: .
(Oxygen is obtained from trees.
Oxygen is obtained from the trees.)

Past Tenses in Sinhala

Now let us learn how to say what happened in the past (that is, we are now going to learn about past tense). Only the verb is modified to form the past time of the tense we have been learning and using so far.

There is a set of rules to show how the verb is modified (or how the past tense derived from the verb root). However, as I have mentioned several times before too, the easy way out is to know a few verbs and identify the simple patterns yourself. Following is a list of some verbs in present and past tense in comparison.

Verb (present)	Verb (past)	Meaning (past)
karanava:	**kala: / keruva:**	did
ma:ru karanava:	**ma:ru kala:/keruva:**	changed, exchanged
sellam karanava:	**sellam kala:/keruva:**	played
kalavam karanava:	**kalavam kala:/keruva:**	mixed
katha: karanava:	**katha: kala:/keruva:**	talked
venava:	**vuna:**	was/were (as in "it was good"), became, happened
thuva:la venava:	**thuva:la vuna:**	hurt, injured

narak venava:	**narak vuna:**	spoilt, rotted, decayed, became bad
loku venava:	**loku vuna:**	grew
hina: venava:	**hina: vuna:**	laughed
nathara venava:	**nathara vuna:**	stopped (as in "the car stopped.")
nathara karanava:	**nathara vuna:**	stopped (as in "I stopped the car.")
innava:	**hitiya:**	was/were (as in "I was in the class room")
thiyenava:	**thibuna:**	had
dhamanava:	**dhaemma:**	put (past)
kapanava:	**kaepuva:**	cut (past)
yanava:	**giya:**	went
enava:	**a:va:**	came
dhenava:	**dhunna:**	gave
gannava:	**gaththa:**	took
hi'mda gannava:	**hi'mda gaththa:**	sat
patan gannava:	**patan gaththa:**	started
balanava:	**baeluva:**	looked
dakinava:	**daekka:**	saw
liyanava:	**livva:**	wrote

kiyavanava:	**kiyevva:**	read (past)
kanava:	**kae:va:**	ate
hadhanava:	**haedhuva:**	made
hithanava:	**hithuva:**	thought
kadanava:	**kaeduva:**	broke
baninava:	**baenna:**	scolded
a'mdanava:	**ae'mduva:**	cried

A large number of common verbs end with *"**karanava**"*, *"**venava**"* (like, *"sellam karanava:"*, *"thuva:la venava:"*) so they all change in the same way.

Initially, you may feel that Sinhala has many irregular verbs (English has around 160 irregular verbs). Definitely, you will notice nice and easy patterns while you keep memorizing the verbs.

> **mama e:ka kala: .**
> (I did it.)
>
> **eya: bath kae:va: .**
> (He ate rice.)
>
> **api hodhi ekka pa:n kae:va: .**
> (We ate bread with curry.)
>
> **gahak kaepuva: .**
> (A tree was cut.)

Let us see how to construct the other variants of this positive statement. Constructing the positive question is very easy; just append "-**dha**" at the end of the past tense verb as usual.

> **mama e:ka kala:dha?**
> (Did I do it?)

> **eya: bath kae:va:dha?**
> (Did he/she eat rice?)

> **api hodhi ekka pa:n kae:va:dha?**
> (Did we eat bread with curry?)

> **gahak kaepuva:dha?**
> (Was a tree cut?)

To make the negative statement, put "*naehae*" after the past tense verb. In addition, you have to change the verb form a bit like this. The ending "a:" vowel sound is changed to "**e:**".

> **mama e:ka kale: naehae.**
> (I did not do it.)

> **eya: bath kae:ve: naehae.**
> (He/She did not eat rice.)

> **api hodhi ekka pa:n kae:ve: naehae.**
> (We did not eat bread with curry.)

> **gahak kaepuwe: naehae.**
> (A tree was not cut.)

To make the negative question, as usual you just change "*nahae*" of the negative statement to "***naedhdha***".

mama e:ka kale: naedhdha?
(Did I not do it?)

eya: bath kae:ve: naedhdha?
(Did she/he not eat rice?)

api hodhi ekka pa:n kae:ve: naedhdha?
(Did we not eat bread with curry?)

gahak kaepuwe: naedhdha?
(Was a tree not cut?)

In the same way you have learnt before, you can construct the two tag questions.

mama e:ka kala: ne:dha?
(I did it. Didn't I?)

eya: bath kae:ve: naehae ne:dha?
(She/He ate rice. Didn't she?)

api hodhi ekka pa:n kae:va: ne:dha?
(We ate bread with curry. Didn't we?)

gahak kaepuwa: ne:dha?
(A tree was cut. Wasn't it?)

In sinhala, some verbs denote a deliberate action (by the doer) like *yanava:* (go), *enava:* (come), *karanava:* (do). Let us call this first category of verbs **"intentional verbs"**. Some verbs denote some indeliberate/unintentional action like *vaetenava:* (fall), *maerenava:* (die), *laebenava:* (get). Let us call this second category of verbs **"automatic verbs"**. You must already have seen that almost all automatic verbs end with **"-enava"**.

Adjectives Formed out of Verbs

Now let us learn how to make an adjective out of a verb -
actually two adjectives. In English too, you have these two
adjectives made in the same way.

You take a "-nava:" verb, and just remove the ending "va:"
syllable. That will be a word behaving like an adjective now.
The meaning is similar to present participle (as an adjective) in
English.

> *karanava:* → **karana** *(doing)*
>
> *balanava:* → **balana** *(looking)*
>
> *kanava:* → **kana** *(eating)*
>
> *yanava:* → **yana** *(going)*
>
> *vaetenava:* → **vaetena** *(falling)*

The other form of adjective is constructed by removing the "-
nava:" ending of the verb (intentional verb), and then appending
"**-pu**" to it. The meaning is similar to the past participle (as an
adjective) in English.

> *karanava:* → **karapu** *(done)*
>
> *balanava:* → **balapu** *(looked)*
>
> *kanava:* → **ka:pu** *(eaten)*
>
> *soyanava:* → **soyapu** *(sought)*

If it is an automatic verb (described above), then you remove "enava:" and append "-**unu**" or "-**ichcha**".

> vaet~~enava:~~ → **vaetunu** or **vaetichcha** *(fallen)*
>
> v~~enava:~~ → **vunu** or **vechcha** *(become, happened)*
>
> maer~~enava:~~ → **maerunu** or **maerichcha** *(dead, died)*
>
> kad~~enava:~~ → **kaedunu** or **kaedichcha** *(broken)*
>
> ipadh~~enava:~~ → **ipadhunu** or **ipadhichcha** *(born)*

There are some irregular instances too. Following is a list of such irregular forms.

> bonava: → **bi:pu** *(drunk)*
>
> yanava: → **gihipu** *(gone)*
>
> gannava: → **gaththu, ganipu** *(taken)*
>
> dhenava: → **dhi:pu** *(given)*
>
> dhakinava: → **dhaekapu** *(seen)*
>
> arinava: → **aerapu** *(opened)*

Let us make some sentences using such adjectives.

> <u>a'ndana</u> lamaya: toffee kanava: .
> (The <u>crying</u> child eats / is eating toffees.)
>
> <u>sellam karana</u> lamai dhaen yanava: .
> (The <u>playing</u> children are going now.)

a'ndapu lamaya: dhaen hina:venava: .
(The cried child is laughing now.)

vaetichcha/vaetunu gaha geniyanava: .
(The fallen tree is carried.)

aerapu dhora vahanna.
(Close the opened door.)

gaththu potha lassanai.
(The book that was taken is beautiful.)

Eya: elavanne: repair karapu va:hanayak.
(He is driving a repaired vehicle.)

Vatichcha mal suva'ndhai.
(The fallen flowers are fragrant.)

liyapu rachana:va neavatha liyanna.
(Write again the written essay.)

Continual Tense

We are now going to learn another important tense in Sinhala. Some grammarians say this is equivalent to the continuous tense in English. There is similarity of course, but I see more than that. It is "richer" than the English continuous tense (so, I call this tense "**continual tense**"). That is, the English continuous tense says something happening at a particular moment, and so is this Sinhala continual tense.

However, Sinhala continual tense gives the impression that the action continues on and on. In English, the meaning is closer to "keep doing".

To make this continual tense verb, you first remove "-nava:" from the "nava:" verb, and suffix "-**min**" to it. After this newly constructed "-min verb", you must put "*innava:*" or "*sitinava:*".

> **...nava: → ...min innava:**
>
> **...nava: → ...min sitinava:**

Karanava: → *karamin innava: / karamin sitinava:* (am/is/are doing or keep doing)

Natanava: → *natamin innava:* (am/is/are dancing or keep dancing)

Kanava: → *kamin innava:* (am/is/are eating or keep eating)

Sellam karanava: → **sellam karamin innava:** *(am/is/are playing or keep plaing)*

Kaehae gahanava: → **kaehae gahamin innava:** *(am/is/are shouting or keep shouting)*

There is another form of the continual tense too. To make that, you remove "-nava:" as usual, and you double the remaining verb part. After that, you put "*innava:*" or "*sitinava:*". The second repeating verb part may take a long vowel at the end.

…nava: → … … innava:

…nava: → … … sitinava:

Karanava: → **kara kara innava: / kara kara: innava:** *(am/is/are doing or keep doing)*

Natanava: → **nata nata sitinava:** *(am/is/are dancing or keep dancing)*

Kanava: → **ka ka: innava:** *(am/is/are eating or keep eating)*

Sellam karanava: → **sellam kara kara innava:** *(am/is/are playing or keep playing)*

Kaehae gahanava: → **kaehae gaha gaha innava:** *(am/is/are shouting or keep shouting)*

Now let us make some sentences with the continual tense. As you can clearly see, even the continual tense verb has a "nava:" verb (*innava:*) in it.

> **Amma: bath uyamin innava: /sitinava:.**
> **Amma: bath uya uya innava: /sitinava:.**
> (The mother is cooking rice. Or the mother keeps cooking.)

> **Mama potha liyamin innava: .**
> **Mama potha liya liya innava: .**
> (I am writing the book. Or I keep writing the book.)

> **Lamai pittaniye: sellam karamin innava: .**
> **Lamai pittaniye: sellam kara kara innava:**
> (Children are playing in the playground.)

Past and Future of Continual Tense

Now you can easily form the past and future times of the continual tense by applying the rules you have already learned.

The continual tense verb has "*innava:*" (or "*sitinava:*"), and therefore it can be regarded as a normal "nava:" verb when you are to modify the verb. Thus, the past tense is formed simply by using the past tense form of the "*innava:*" verb (that is, "***hitiya:***"), and the future tense by using the future tense form of it (that is, "***hi'ndhi:vi***").

kara kara innava:/sitinava: → kara kara hitiya:
karamin innava:/sitinava: → karamin hitiya:

kara kara innava:/sitinava: → kara kara hi'ndhi:vi
karamin innava:/sitinava: → karamin hi'ndhi:vi

*Kara kara innava: /sitinava: → **kara kara hitiya:***
(was/were doing or kept doing)
*karamin innava: /sitinava: → **karamin hitiya:***
(was/were doing or kept doing)

*Uyamin innava: → **uyamin hitiya:** (was/were cooking or*
kept cooking)
*Uya uya innava: → **uya uya hitiya:** (was/were cooking*
or kept cooking)

*Kara kara innava: → **kara kara hi'ndhi:vi** (will be*
doing or will keep doing)
*Karamin innava: → **karamin hi'ndhi:vi** (will be doing*
or will keep doing)

*Uyamin innava: → **uyamin hi'ndhi:vi** (will be cooking*
or will keep cooking)
*Uya uya innava: → **uya uya hi'ndhi:vi** (will be cooking*
or will keep cooking)

Let us make some sentences in past and future times of the
continual tense. From this moment on, I will just write the
English continuous form only to give the meaning of Sinhala
continual tense.

Balla: i:ye bura bura hitiya: .
Balla: i:ye buramin hitiya: .
(The dog was barking yesterday.)

Lamai sellam kara kara hitiya: .
Lamai sellam karamin hitiya: .
(The children were playing.)

Eya: geyak hada hada hi'ndhi:vi.
Eya: geyak hadamin hi'ndhi:vi.
(He/She will be building a house.)

Nangi dhavasema a'ndamin hi'ndhi:vi.
Nangi dhavasema a'nda a'nda hi'ndhi:vi.
(Younger sister will be crying the whole day.)

You must know how to make other variants (negative statement, questions, tag questions) of this tense in all three times (present, past, future). It is not difficult at all because once again you have to simply follow the rules you already know.

Negative Statements and Questions

In addition to the usual sentence pattern for the negative variants (that is, negative statement and negative question), there is another popular method. Here, we use *"neme:"* or *"nemei"* (instead of *"naehae"*), and put it just before the *"inne:"* or *"hitiye:"*. And in the case of negative question, you append "-dha" (which denotes a question) to the *"neme:"* (like *"neme:dha"*). Carefully see the following examples.

Amma: bath uyamin inne: naehae.
Amma: bath uyamin neme: inne: .
(The mother is not cooking rice.)

Amma: bath uya uya inne: naehae.
Amma: bath uya uya neme: inne: .
(The mother is not cooking rice.)

Mama potha liyamin/liya liya inne: naehae.
Mama potha liyamin/liya liya neme: inne: .
(I am not writing the book.)

Amma: bath uyamin/uya uya hitiye: naehae.
Amma: bath uyamin/uya uya neme: hitiye: .
(The mother was not cooking rice.)

Mama potha liyamin/liya liya hitiye: naehae.
Mama potha liyamin/liya liya neme: hitiye: .
(I was not writing the book.)

Amma: bath uyamin/uya uya inna ekak naehae.
(The mother will not be cooking rice.)

Mama potha liyamin/liya liya inna ekak naehae.
(I will not be writing the book.)

Amma: bath uyamin/uya uya inne: naedhdha?
Amma: bath uyamin/uya uya neme:dha inne:?
(Is the mother not cooking rice?)

Mama potha liyamin/liya liya inne: naedhdha?
Mama potha liyamin/liya liya neme:dha inne?
(Am I not writing the book?)

Amma: bath uyamin/uya uya hitiye: naedhdha?
Amma: bath uyamin/uya uya neme:dha hitiye:?
(Was the mother not cooking rice?)

Mama potha liyamin/liya liya hitiye: naedhdha?
Mama potha liyamin/liya liya neme:dha hitiye:?
(Was I not writing the book?)

Amma: bath uyamin/uya uya inna ekak naedhdha?
(Will the mother not be cooking rice?)

Mama potha liyamin/liya liya inna ekak naedhdha?
(Will I not be writing the book?)

Positive questions

Here too, we have another popular form. You just suffix
question-making "-dha" to the "min verb" or its other alternative
as follows. Then, *"innava:"* is changed to *"inne:"*, and *"hitiya:"*
to *"hitiye:"*.

Amma: bath uyamin innava:dha?
Amma: bath uyamindha inne:?
(Is the mother cooking?)

Amma: bath uya uya innava:dha?
Amma: bath uya uyadha inne:?
(Is the mother cooking?)

Mama potha liyamin innava:dha?
Mama potha liyamindha inne:?
(Am I writing the book?)

Mama potha liya liya innava:dha?
Mama potha liya liyadha inne:?
(Am I writing the book?)

Amma: bath uyamin hitiya:dha?
Amma: bath uyamindha hitiye:?
(Was the mother cooking rice?)

Amma: bath uya uya hitiya:dha?
Amma: bath uya uyadha hitiye:?
(Was the mother cooking rice?)

Mama potha liyamin hitiya:dha?
Mama potha liyamindha hitiye:?
(Was I writing the book?)

Mama potha liya liya hitiya:dha?
Mama potha liya liyadha hitiye:?
(Was I writing the book?)

Amma: bath uyamin/uya uya hi'ndhi:vidha?
(Will the mother be cooking?)

Mama potha liyamin/liya liya hi'ndhi:vidha?
(Will I be writing the book?)

Tag questions

Again, there is the usual alternative form here too. You put
"*ne:dha*" just before "*inne:*" or "*hitiye:*"

> **Amma: bath uyamin/uya uya innava: ne:dha?**
> **Amma: bath uyamin/uya uya ne:dha inne:?**
> (The mother is cooking rice. Isn't she?)

> **Mama potha liyamin/liya liya inne naehae ne:dha?**
> **Mama potha liyamin/liya liya neme: ne:dha inne:?**
> (I am not writing the book. Am I?)

> **Amma: bath uyamin/uya uya hitiye: naeahe ne:dha?**
> **Amma: bath uyamin/uya uya neme: ne:dha hitiye:?**
> (The mother was not cooking rice. Was she?)

> **Mama potha liyamin/liya liya hitiya: ne:dha?**
> **Mama potha liyamin/liya liya ne:dha hitiye:?**
> (I was writing the book. Wasn't I?)

> **Amma: bath uyamin/uya uya hi'ndhi:vi ne:dha?**
> (The mother will be cooking rice. Won't she?)

> **Mama potha liyamin/liya liya inna ekak naehae
> ne:dha?**
> (I will not be writing the book. Will I?)

"BE-sentences" in Sinhala

In most languages, there is a special sentence structure where you cannot see a distinct action. For example, when you say "*I am running*" or "*I run*" or "*I have run*", you have some action (that is, "the action of running") in it. However, when you say "*I am good*" or "*He is a doctor*" or "*We are in the class*", there you can't see any action.

These "actionless sentences" are constructed with "**BE**" (am/is/are) in English. Now let us see how it is done in Sinhala. Here we are going to learn how to write Sinhala sentences corresponding to the English sentences using the BE verb.

I will explain it with respect to English "be" sentence structure; it will be much easier then. **In English, you write it in one of three ways.**

1. **After the verb "be", you have an adjective (quality).**

   For example:

   > *I am good.*
   > *She is beautiful.*
   > *They are kind.*

   In Sinhala, you can very easily make the equivalent sentence just by writing the doer first, then the adjective (quality that the doer possesses), and after that "-**yi**" is appened to the adjective. This "-yi" is similar in function to the "be" verb in English.

Mama ho'ndhayi.

(I am good.)

Eya: lassanayi.

(She is beautiful.)

Egollo karuna:vanthayi.

(They are kind.)

Positive Question

Let us learn how to make the other variants of this sentence. To form the postive question, you just put "-dha" at the end of adjective ending with "-yi". If you like, you can remove "-yi" when appending "dha".

Mama ho'ndhayidha?
Mama ho'ndhadha?
(Am I good?)

Eya: lassanayidha?
Eya: lassanadha?
(Is she beautiful?)

Egollo karuna:vanthayidha?
Egollo karuna:vanthadha?
(Are they kind?)

Negative Statement and Question

To make the negative statement of these, you simply put
"*naehae*" after the adjective, and while doing so, remove
"-yi" too.

> **Mama ho'ndha naehae.**
> (I am not good.)

> **Eya: lassana naehae.**
> (She is not beautiful.)

> **Egollo karuna:vantha naehae.**
> (They are not kind.)

To form the negative question, just substitute "*naedhdha*"
for "*naehae*" above.

> **Mama ho'ndha naedhdha?**
> (Am I not good?)

> **Eya: lassana naedhdha?**
> (Is she not beautiful?)

> **Egollo karuna:vantha naedhdha?**
> (Are they not kind?)

Tag Questions

Now let us see how tag questions are formed. Simply put "*ne:dha*" at the end of the positive or negative statements above.

> **Mama ho'ndhai ne:dha?**
> (I am good. Aren't I?)
> **Mama ho'ndha naehae ne:dha?**
> (I am not good. Am I?)
>
> **Eya: lassanai ne:dha?**
> (She is beautiful. Isn't she?)
> **Eya: lassana naehae ne:dha?**
> (She is not beautiful. Is she?)

2. **After the "be" verb, you may have a noun.**

For example:

> *I am a child.*
> *I am the child.*
> *He is a sportsman.*
> *We are teachers.*

In Sinhala, you can make these sentences first putting the doer as usual, and then just placing the noun (definte or indefinite) after that. That's it.

> **Mama lamayek.**
> (I am a child.)

Mama lamaya: .
(I am the child.)

Eya: kri:dakayek.
(He is a sportsman.)

Api guruvaru/teacherla: .
(We are teachers.)

Deriving other variants is as usual. Let us see a few examples of them.

Mama lamayek neme: .
(I am not a child.)
Mama lamayekdha?
(Am I a child?)
Mama lamayek ne:dha?
(I am a child. Aren't I?)
Mama lamayek neme: ne:dha?
(I am not a child. Am I?)

Mama lamaya: neme: .
(I am not the child.)
Mama lamaya:dha?
(Am I the child?)
Mama lamaya: neme:dha?
(Am I not the child?)
Mama lamaya: ne:dha?
(I am the child. Aren't I?)

Mama lamaya: neme: ne:dha?
(I am not the child. Am I?)

Eya: kri:dakayek neme: .
(He is not a sportsman.)
Eya: kri:dakayekdha?
(Is he a sportsman?)
Eya: kri:dakayek neme:dha?
(Is he not a sportsman?)
Eya: kri:dakayek ne:dha?
(He is a sportsman. Isn't he?)
Eya: kri:dakayek neme: ne:dha?
(He is not a sportsman. Is he?)

3. **After the "be" verb, you have a preposition** (and connected noun).

   This includes "there is/are" sentence structure too. For example:

   I am in the class.
   She is at the gate.
   We are on the road.
   There is a bird on the roof.

   In Sinhala, making these sentences is not so easy as above two, but this is not very difficult either. First say the doer, and then say the preposition and its noun as you normally say in Sinhala (we learned this earlier).

Optionally you can put "inne:" after the prepositional part (ie, preposition and its noun), or before the prepositional part.

> **Mama panthiye:/panthiya thula.**
> **Mama panthiye:/panthiya thula inne: .**
> **Mama inne: panthiye:/panthiya thula.**
> (I am in the class.)

> **Eya: ge:ttuva la'nga.**
> **Eya: ge:ttuva la'nga inne: .**
> **Eya: inne: ge:ttuva la'nga.**
> (She is at the gate.)

> **Api pa:re:/pa:ra uda.**
> **Api pa:re:/pa:ra uda inne: .**
> **Api inne: pa:re:/pa:ra uda.**
> (We are on the road.)

To make the negative statement, you just put "*naehae*" or "*neme:*" after the prepositional part.

Append "-dha" to the prepositional part to form the postive question.

To make the negative question, put "*naedhdha*" or "*neme:dha*" to the positive statement.

Tag questions are formed as usual.

Study the following examples well, and you will see the patterns (the same set of patterns you had seen before). If there is "*inne:*" in the sentence, then that part comes last.

Mama panthiye: naehae/neme: .
Mama panthiya thula naehae/neme: .
Mama panthiye:/panthiya thula neme inne.
Mama inne: panthiye/panthiya thula neme.
(I am not in the class.)

Eya: ge:ttuva la'nga naehae/neme: .
Eya: ge:ttuva la'nga neme inne: .
Eya: inne: ge:ttuva la'nga neme: .
(She is not at the gate.)

Mama panthiye:dha?
Mama panthiya thuladha?
Mama panthiye:/panthiya thula innavadha?
Mama inne panthiye:dha/panthiya thuladha?
(Am I in the class?)

Eya: ge:ttuva la'nga neme:dha?
Eya: ge:ttuva la'nga neme:dha inne?
Eya: inne ge:ttuva la'nga neme:dha?
(Is she not at the gate?)

Api pa:re:/pa:ra uda ne:dha?
Api pa:re:/pa:ra uda ne:dha inne:?
Api inne: pa:re:/pa:ra uda ne:dha?
(We are on the road. Aren't we?)

Api pa:re:/pa:ra uda neme: ne:dha?
Api pa:re:/pa:ra uda neme: ne:dha inne?

Api inne: pa:re:/pa:ra uda neme: ne:dha?
(We are not on the road. Are we?)

Vahalaya matha/Vahalaye: kurullek naehae.
(There is not a bird on the roof.)

**Vahalaya matha/Vahalaye: kurullek
innavadha?**
(Is there a bird on the roof?)

Vahalaya matha/Vahalaye: kurullek naedhdha?
(Is there not a bird on the roof?)

Forming Verbs out of Adjectives

There are two nice and short methods to make verbs out of adjectives in Sinhala. Even in English, you can do the same (to make a verb out of an adjective using "make" or "get/become"). However, most if not all the Sinhala verbs constructed like this are independent valid verbs on their own.

If you add "*karanava:*" after an adjective, you get a verb as follows. As you can see, it has "**make *adjective***" as the English meaning. The type of verb formed this way is an intentional verb (doing something intentionally).

> *Lassana (beautiful) → **lassana karanava:** (make beautiful, beautify, decorate)*
>
> *Kaetha (ugly) → **kaetha karanava:** (make ugly, disfigure, tarnish)*
>
> *Dhiga (long) → **dhiga karanava:** (make long, lengthen)*
>
> *Kota (short) → **kota karanava:** (make short, shorten, abbreviate)*
>
> *Kalavam (mixed) → **kalavam karanava:** (make mixed, mix)*
>
> *Sathutu (happy) → **sathutu karanava:** (make merry, amuse)*
>
> *Sudhu (white) → **sudhu karanava:** (make white, whiten)*
>
> *Kalu (black) → **kalu karanava:** (make black, blacken, make dark)*

Another way to make a verb out of an adjective is to add
"*venava:*" after the adjective. The English meaning is like
"**become/get** *adjective*". The type of verb formed in this way is
an automatic verb (doing without a purpose).

> *Lassana (beautiful)* → **lassana venava:** *(become
> beautiful)*
>
> *Kaetha (ugly)* → **kaetha venava:** *(become ugly)*
>
> *Dhiga (long)* → **dhiga venava:** *(become long)*
>
> *Kota (short)* → **kota venava:** *(become short)*
>
> *Sathutu (happy)* → **sathutu venava:** *(get happy, have fun,
> enjoy)*
>
> *Sudhu (white)* → **sudhu venava:** *(become white, become
> fair-complexioned)*
>
> *Kalu (black)* → **kalu venava:** *(become black, become
> dark-complexioned)*

These two methods are used to make Sinhala verbs out of
Sinhala nouns; and to make Sinhala verbs out of English nouns
or verbs or adjectives too (these English nouns/verbs/adjectives
are popular or common among Sinhala speakers).

However, you cannot make verbs from every Sinhala noun or
every English noun/verb/adjective. Because we re-use the same
word, you can easily increase your working vocabulary with this.

> *Sellam (games)* → **sellam karanava:** *(do games, play)*
>
> *Katha: (talks)* → **katha: karanava:** *(talk)*

Chu: (urine) → **chu: karanava:** *(urinate)*

Dhaduvam (punishments) → **dhaduvam karanava:** *(punish)*

Sex → **sex karanava:** *(have sex)*

Powder → **powder karanava:** *(grind to powder, powder)*

On → **on karanava:** *(turn on)*

Off → **off karanava:** *(turn off)*

Ready → **ready karanava:** *(make ready)*

Short → **short karanava:** *(make short, shorten)*

Fit → **fit karanava:** *(fit)*

Flat → **flat karanava:** *(flatten)*

Seal → **seal karanava:** *(seal)*

Support → **support karanava:** *(support)*

Check → **check karanava:** *(check)*

Kiss → **kiss karanava:** *(kiss)*

Try → **try karanava:** *(try)*

Repair → **repair karanava:** *(repair)*

Plan → **plan karanava:** *(plan)*

Play → **play karanava:** *(play)*

Call → **call karanava:** *(make calls, call)*

Ring → **ring karanava:** *(ring)*

Drive → **drive karanava:** *(drive)*

Pack → **pack karanava:** *(pack)*

Type → **type karanava:** *(type)*

Test → **test karanava:** *(test)*

Study → **study karanava:** *(study)*

Print → **print karanava:** *(print)*

Set → **set karanava:** *(set, match)*

If you want to say that something occurs by itself (automatically), or that something is done by something/somebody, then you can use "venava:" with **suitable** English verbs/nouns/adjectives.

Print → **print venava:** *(be/get printed)*

Set → **set venava:** *(be/get matched)*

Type → **type venava:** *(be/get typed)*

Play → **play venava:** *(be/get played)*

Check → **check venava:** *(be/get checked)*

On → **on venava:** *(be/get switched on, become on)*

Off → **off venava:** *(be/get switched off, become off)*

Fit – **fit venava:** *(be/get fit, become fit, fit)*

Actually, the above methods of making verbs out of English verbs/nouns/adjectives are very popular and common when using technical words.

Even though Sinhala language has pure Sinhala technical words, they are just ignored because higher and professional education in Sri Lanka is carried out in English medium. On the other, almost all books are in English.

There is a funny saying - *you can easily speak Sinhala just by putting "karanava:" after each English words and "eka" after each English noun.*

Now let us make several sentences with those verbs. In addition, you can other variants (negative statement, questions, etc) very easily too.

> **Eya: gedhara malvalin lassana karanava: .**
> (He decorates the house with flowers.)
>
> **Lamaya: liyumak type karanava: .**
> (The child types a letter.)
>
> **E:ka check karanna epa: .**
> (Don't check it.)
>
> **Oya: ana:gathaya plan karanna.**
> (You plan the future.)
>
> **Dhaen TV eka off karanna.**
> (Now turn off the TV.)
>
> **Me: bulb eka me: holder ekata fit venne: naehae.**
> (This bulb does fit to/with this holder.)

Infinitives

Just as in English, where we construct the **infinitive** by putting "to" in front of an English verb, we can make the infinitive in Sinhala too. Then the "nava:" part of the "-nava:" verb is substituted with "-**nnata**".

Often, you can do away with the "-ta" part too. If you like, you can also use "-**nda**" instead of "-nnata".

$$...\text{nava:} \rightarrow ...\text{nnata}$$
$$...\text{nava:} \rightarrow ...\text{nna}$$
$$...\text{nava:} \rightarrow ...\text{nda}$$

Karanava: → **karannata , karanna, karanda** *(to do)*

Kanava: → **kannata, kanna, kanda** *(to eat)*

Bonava: → **bonnata, bonna, bonda** *(to drink)*

Wherever there is a verb in whatever form, it has the right to get an *object* (if possible), *adverbs*, or *prepositional parts*.

It is same in Sinhala too. Thus, the verb in the infinitive can take any or all of them. In Sinhala, object, adverb, or prepositional part comes before the verb (that means here too the usual word order is maintained).

Kanava:

→ **bath** **kanna/kannata/kanda** *(to eat rice)*

→ **ikmanin** **kanna/kannata/kanda** *(to eat quickly)*

→ **panthiye:** **kanna/kannata/kanda** *(to eat in the class)*

→ **panthiye: ikmanin bath** **kanna/kannata/kanda** *(to eat rice quickly in the class)*

Now let us make sentences with infinitives. Where in the sentence to put the infinitive? It is put before the main verb.

Mama kanna yanava: .

(I am going to eat.)

Mama bath kanna yanava: .

(I am going to eat rice.)

Mama ikmanin kanna yanava: .

(I am going to eat quickly.)

Mama panthiye: kanna yanava: .

(I am going to eat in the class.)

Mama bath ikmanin kanna yanava:.

(I am going to eat rice quickly.)

Eya: bath kanna yanne: naehae.

(He is not going to eat rice.)

Shane dhuvanna neme: sithuve.

(Shane did not think to run.)

To make the positive question, you can put "-dha" at the end of
the verb as usual. Or you can put "-dha" at the end of the
infinitive too; then the main "nava:" verb is changed to "nne:".

> **Eya: bath kanna yanava:dha?**
> **Eya: bath kannadha yanne:?**
> (Is he going to eat rice?)

> **Api football sellam karanna yanava:dha?**
> **Api football sellam karannadha yanne:?**
> (Are we going to play football?)

> **Eya: e:ka kadanna try karanava:dha?**
> **Eya: e:ka kadannadha try karanne:?**
> (Is he trying to break it?)

> **Dhaen api pa:dam karanna ready vemudha?**
> (Shall we be ready to study now?)

To make the negative question, you can put *"neme:dha"* after
the infinitive and change the "nava: verb to "nne:". Or you can
put *"naedhdha"* after the main verb, and change the verb to
"nne:".

> **Eya: bath kanna neme:dha yanne:?**
> **Eya: bath kanna yanne: naedhdha?**
> (Is he not going to eat rice?)

> **Eya: e:ka kadanna neme:dha try karanne:?**
> **Eya: e:ka kadanna try karanne: naedhdha?**
> (Is he not trying to break it?)

In English, there is "**be going to**" sentence structure to say
something is going to happen in the future. Sinhala too has the

same sentence structure in the same meaning. You already saw this in above examples. It is "... *yanava:*" or "... *yanne:*" or "*inne:*" or "... *hadhanne:*" or "... *hadhanava:*". In this sentence structure too, we use infinitive.

> **Mama sinduvak kiyanna**
> **yanava:/yanne:/hadhanne:/hadhanava: .**
> (I am going to sing.)
>
> **Api uyanna hadanne:/yanne:/yanava:/hadhanava: .**
> (We are going to cook.)
>
> **Amma: malli ge:nna hadhanav:dha?**
> (Is the mother going to take the younger brother?)

Perfect Tense in Sinhala

In Sinhala, too you can find **perfect tense**. It is very similar to English Perfect tense both in meaning and in the way the perfect tense verb is constructed.

First take the "-nava:" verb and remove that "nava:" part, and then append "-**la:**" or "-**la**" to it. Thereafter, you have to put "*thiyenava:*" (in the present time), "*thibuna:*" (in the past time), or "*thiye:vi*" (in the future time) after the "- la:" verb participle.

…nava: → …la thiyenava:

…nava: → …la thibuna:

…nava: → …la thiye:vi

Karanava:
  → *karala: thiyenava:* (have done)
  → *karala: thibuna:* (had done)
  → *karala: thiye:vi* (will have done)

Sellam karanava: → **sellam karala: thiyenava:** (have played)

Balanava: → **balala: thiyenava:** (have looked)

Venava: → **vela: thiyenava:** (have become/happened)

Hina: venava: → **hina: vela: thiyenava:** (have laughed)

Natanava: → **natala: thiyenava:** (have danced)

Allanava: → **allala: thiyenava:** (have touched/caught)

When the verb ends with "inava:", then that part is removed, and "-la:" is appended to it. In addition, if that verb's first syllable **rhymes like** "X<u>a</u>", then that part is changed to "X<u>ae</u>" too.

Baninava: → ***baenala: thiyenava:*** *(have scolded)*

Kahinava: → ***kaehala: thiyenava:*** *(have coughed)*

Bahinava: → ***baehala: thiyenava:*** *(have descended/lowered)*

Paninava: → ***paenala: thiyenava:*** *(have jumped)*

Dhakinava: → ***dhaekala: thiyenava:*** *(have seen)*

Isinava: → ***isala: thiyenava:*** *(have sprinkled)*

Hi'nbinava: → ***hi'nbala: thiyenava:*** *(have kissed/sniffed)*

When the verb ends with "enava:", then that part is removed, and "-i:la:" is appended to it.

Dhenava: → ***dhi:la: thiyenava:*** *(have given)*

Pipenava: → ***pipi:la: thiyenava:*** *(have bloomed/blossomed)*

Penenava: → ***penila: thiyenava:*** *(have seen)*

Dhaenenava: → ***dhaenila: thiyenava:*** *(have felt)*

Naemenava: → ***naemila: thiyenava:*** *(have been bent)*

There are some exceptions too (small modifications in the verb) as follows.

Kanava: → **ka:la: thiyenava:** (have eaten)

Bonava: → **bi:la: thiyenava:** (have drunk)

Yanava: → **gihilla: thiyenava:** (have gone)

Enava: → **avilla: thiyenava:** (have come)

Gannava: → **aran thiyenava:** (have taken)

Gena:va: → **genath/genalla: thiyenava:** (have brought)

Now let us make some perfect tense sentences.

Mama e:ka karala: thiyenava: .
(I have done it.)

Eya: me:ka dhaekala: thiyenava: .
(He/She has seen this.)

Api football sellam karala: thiyenava: .
(We have played football.)

Gaha kapala: thiyenava: .
(The tree has been cut.)

Past and Future of Perfect Tense

You can make past and future time sentences of this perfect tense easily with the knowledge you have obtained by now. In the past tense, *"thiyenava:"* part of the perfect tense is substituted with *"**thibuna:**"*.

In the future tense, *"thiyenava:"* part is replaced with *"**thiye:vi**"*.

Mama e:ka karala: thibuna: .
(I had done it.)

Eya: me:ka dhaekala: thibuna: .

(He/She had seen this.)

Api football sellam karala: thibuna: .

(We had played football.)

Gaha kapala: thibuna: .

(The tree had been cut.)

Mama e:ka karala: thiye:vi.

(I will have done it.)

Eya: me:ka dhaekala: thiye:vi.

(He/She will have seen this.)

Api football sellam karala: thiye:vi.

(We will have played football.)

Gaha kapala: thiye:vi.

(The tree will have been cut.)

Negative Statements

You can now construct the variants of the positive statement of perfect tense. First, let us see how to construct the negative statement. You have to put *"naehae"* after the perfect tense verb. Then, in the present tense you should drop *"thiyenava:"*. In the past tense, you change *"thibuna:"* to *"thibune:"*; and in the future tense, *"thiye:vi"* is changed to *"thiyena ekak"*.

Mama e:ka karala: naehae.

(I have not done it.)

Mama e:ka karala: thibune: naehae.

(I had not done it.)

Mama e:ka karala: thiyena ekak naehae.

(I will not have done it.)

Eya: me:ka dhaekala: naehae.

(She/He has not seen this.)

Eya: me:ka dhaekala: thibune: naehae.

(She/He had not seen this.)

Eya: me:ka dhaekala: thiyena ekak naehae.

(She/He will not have seen this.)

Api football sellam karala: naehae.

(We have not played football.)

Api football sellam karala: thibune: naehae.

(We had not played football.)

Api football sellam karala: thiyena ekak naehae.

(We will not have played football.)

Gaha kapala: naehae.

(The tree has not been cut.)

Gaha kapala: thibune: naehae.

(The tree had not been cut.)

Gaha kapala: thiyena ekak naehae.

(The tree will not have been cut.)

Positive Questions

To make the positive question, simply put "-dha" at the end of the tense verb.

Mama e:ka karala: thiyenava:dha?
(Have I done it?)
Mama e:ka karala: thibuna:dha?
(Had I done it?)
Mama e:ka karala: thiye:vidha?
(Will I have done it?)

Eya: me:ka dhaekala: thiyenava:dha?
(Has she/he seen it?)
Eya: me:ka dhaekala: thibuna:dha?
(Had she/he seen it?)
Eya: me:ka dhaekala: thiye:vidha?
(Will she/he have seen it?)

Api football sellam karala: thiyenava:dha?
(Have we played football?)
Api football sellam karala: thibuna:dha?
(Had we played football?)
Api football sellam karala: thiye:vidha?
(Will we have played football?)

Gaha kapala: thiyenava:dha?
(Has the tree been cut?)
Gaha kapala: thibuna:dha?
(Had the tree been cut?)
Gaha kapala: thiye:vidha?
(Will the tree have been cut?)

Negative Questions

To make the negative question is as same as what you have been learning and practicing so far. You put *"naedhdha"* at the end of the tense verb. In the present tense, you also drop *"thiyenava:"* part. In the past tense, change *"thibuna:"* to *"thibune:"*; and in the future tense, change *"thiye:vi"* into *"thiyena ekak"*.

Mama e:ka karala: naedhdha?

(Have I not done it?)

Mama e:ka karala: thibune: nadhdha?

(Had I not done it?)

Mama e:ka karala: thiyena ekak naedhdha?

(Will I not have done it?)

Eya: me:ka dhaekala: naedhdha?

(Has she/he not seen this?)

Eya: me:ka dhaekala: thibune: naedhdha?

(Had she/he not seen this?)

Eya: me:ka dhaekala: thiyena ekak naedhdha?

(Will she/he not have seen this?)

Api football sellam karala: naedhdha?

(Have we not played football?)

Api football sellam karala: thibune: naedhdha?

(Had we not played football?)

Api football sellam karala: thiyena ekak naedhdha?

(Will we not have played football?)

Gaha kapala: naedhdha?

(Has the tree not been cut?)

Gaha kapala: thibune: naedhdha?

(Had the tree not been cut?)

Gaha kapala: thiyena ekak naedhdha?

(Will the tree not have been cut?)

Tag Questions

There is nothing new in making the tag questions.

Mama e:ka karala: thiyenava: ne:dha?

(I have done it. Haven't I?)

Mama e:ka karala: naehae ne:dha?

(I have not done it. Have I?)

Mama e:ka karala: thibuna: ne:dha?

(I had done it. Hadn't I?)

Mama e:ka karala: thibune: naehae ne:dha?

(I had not done it. Had I?)

Mama e:ka karala: thiye:vi ne:dha?

(I will have done it. Won't I?)

Mama e:ka karala: thiyena ekak naehae ne:dha?

(I will not have done it. Will I?)

Gaha kapala: ne:dha?

(The tree has been cut. Hasn't it?)

Gaha kapala: thibune: naehae ne:dha?

(The tree had not been cut. Had it?)

Gaha kapala: thiye:vi ne:dha?

(The tree will have been cut. Won't it?)

Sometimes you drop the "*thiyenava:*" part in the present perfect tense in the positive statement form too. It has the same perfect tense meaning, but there is something more there now. You use this form when you want to say a perfect tense statement with a surprise, or with a meaning to the effect that *"it's already done and now you can do nothing about it"* (that is, denoting the completion of the action).

Eya: e:ka ka:la: .
(He has eaten it.)

Lamaya: kiri bi:la: .
(The child has drunk milk.)

Eya: salli di:la: .
(He has given money.)

Match eka paeradila: .
(The match has been lost.)

Prashnaya visadila: .
(The problem has been solved.)

Perfect Continuous Tense in Sinhala

You can make the **perfect continuous tense** in Sinhala too. Not only that, you can make it in both active and passive voices (actually in spoken Sinhala, there is no difference in voices); you might know that in English you cannot make perfect continuous tense sentences in passive voice.

Here, you can easily make the perfect continuous verb by taking the continual tense verb and replace "*innava:*" with "*i'ndhala: thiyenava:*". Very easy!

> **Mama bath kamin/kaka: i'ndhala: thiyenava: .**
> (I have been eating rice.)
> **Mama bath kamin/kaka: i'ndhala: thibuna: .**
> (I had been eating rice.)
> **Mama bath kamin/kaka: i'ndhala: thiye:vi.**
> (I will have been eating rice.)
>
> **Francis potha liyamin/liya liya i'ndhala: thiyenava: .**
> (Francis has been writing the book.)
> **Francis potha liyamin/liya liya i'ndhala: thibuna: .**
> (Francis had been writing the book.)
> **Francis potha liyamin/liya liya i'ndhala: thiye:vi.**
> (Francis will have been writing the book.)
>
> **Gaha kapamin/kapa kapa i'ndhala: thiyenava: .**
> ('*someone*' has been cutting the tree. Or the tree has been being cut.)

Gaha kapamin/kapa kapa i'ndhala: thibuna: .
(*'someone'* had been cutting the tree. Or the tree had been being cut.)

Gaha kapamin/kapa kapa i'ndhala: thiye:vi.
(*'someone'* will have been cutting the tree. Or the tree will have been being cut.)

You can make all the variants just like the perfect tense (because even the perfect continuous tense verb has *"thiyenava:"* at the end).

Mama bath kamin/kaka: i'ndhala: naehae.
(I have not been eating rice.)
Mama bath kamin/kaka: i'ndhala: thiyenava:dha?
(Have I been eating rice?)
Mama bath kamin/kaka: i'ndhala: naedhdha?
(Have I not been eating rice?)
Mama bath kamin/kaka: i'ndhala: thiyenava: ne:dha?
(I have been eating rice. Haven't I?)
Mama bath kamin/kaka: i'ndhala: naehae ne:dha?
(I have not been eating rice. Have I?)

Francis potha liyamin/liya liya i'ndhala: thibune: naehae.
(Francis had not been writing the book.)
Francis potha liyamin/liya liya i'ndhala: thibuna:dha?
(Had Francis been writing the book?)
Francis potha liyamin/liya liya i'ndhala: thibune: naedhdha?
(Had Francis not been writing the book?)

Francis potha liyamin/liya liya i'ndhala: thibuna: ne:dha?

(Francis had been writing the book. Hadn't he?)

Francis potha liyamin/liya liya i'ndhala: thibune: naedhdha?

(Francis had not been writing the book. Had he?)

Now we have covered all the tenses that you find in both Sinhala and English. I strongly suggest you to study and memorize grammar points and patterns well in the lessons in order, without jumping here and there.

Helping Verbs

Now that you know about (plain) tenses, you can learn how to use **helping/auxiliary verbs** with them. There are a few helping verbs in Sinhala.

Put the helping verb after the normal present tense verb.
The tense verb may be modified a little.

Note that tense does not change in structure because in any tense you will find a "nava:" verb at the end (but the effect of tense is there in the meaning indeed).

You can use helping verbs with "be sentences" too. There is a common pattern here. When you use a helping verb with a "be sentence" having an adjective or a noun or a prepositional part, you should include *"viya"* or *"venna/venda/vennata"* just before the helping verb, and you must keep the adjective or noun as is (without any suffix).

Optionally, when you use a helping verb with a "be sentence" having a prepositional part, you should include *"inna/innata/inda"* just before the helping verb. You will understand this more clearly with examples given below.

Let us learn helping verbs one by one.

1. yuthui/o:na/o:ne

– must/should/ought to (required to do something)

The verb's end changes differently for *"yuthui"* and *"o:na"*/*"o:ne"*.

For "*yuthui*", the "Xnava:" part ("X represents any vowel sound) of a "nava:" verb is removed and "**-iya**" is appended. Then, "*yuthui*" is put.

You can put "*o:na*", but the verb is modified to infinitive form of the tense verb (that you learned before). Actually, this form is better because it is easier to make, and some verbs can support this method only.

> *venava:* → **viya yuthui** *or*
> **venna/vennata/venda o:na**
> *(must be/ must happen/ must become)*

> *loku venava:* → **loku viya yuthui** *or*
> **loku venna/venda/vennata o:na**
> *(must grow/must become large)*

> *vaetenava:* → **vaetiya yuthui** *or*
> **vaetenna/vaetenda/vaetennata o:na**
> *(must fall)*

> *selavenava:* → **selaviya yuthui** *or*
> **selavenna/selavenda/selavennata o:na**
> *(must be shaken)*

> *kiyavanava:* → **kiyaviya yuthui** *or*
> **kiyavanna/kiyavanda/kiyavannata o:na**
> *(must read)*

When that "nava:" verb's beginning syllable rhymes like "X<u>a</u>"
(that is, there is a vowel sound "a" after some consonant
represented here by X), then that syllable is changed to "X<u>ae</u>".
After this, you put "*yuthui*".

> p<u>a</u>ninava: → **p<u>ae</u>niya yuthui** *or*
> > **paninna/paninda/paninnata o:na**
>
> *(must jump)*
>
> b<u>a</u>lanava: → **b<u>ae</u>liya yuthui** *or*
> > **balanna/balanda/balannata o:na**
>
> *(must look)*
>
> n<u>a</u>vanava: → **n<u>ae</u>viya yuthui** *or*
> > **navanna/navanda/navannata o:na**
>
> *(must bend)*
>
> b<u>a</u>ninava: → **b<u>ae</u>niya yuthui** *or*
> > **baninna/baninda/baninnata o:na**
>
> *(must scold)*
>
> r<u>a</u>vanava: → **r<u>ae</u>viya yuthui** *or*
> > **ravanna/ravannata/ravanda o:na**
>
> *(must frown)*

If the beginning syllable rhymes like "X<u>o</u>", then it is changed to
"X<u>e</u>". After this, you just put "*yuthui*".

solavanava: → **selaviya yuthui** *or*
                    solavanna/solavanda/solavannata o:na
    (must shake)

hoyanava: → **heviya yuthui** *or*
                    hoyanna/hoyanda/hoyannata o:na
    (must search)

There are irregular forms too. Specially the verb "*karanava:*"
must be remembered because you find thousands of verbs
having it; so all such verbs ending with "*karanava:*" behave in
the same manner. Again remember that the "*o:na*" helping verb
with the infinitive is same everywhere in form; so it is common
and easy.

karanava: → **kala yuthui** *or*
                    karanna/karannata/karanda o:na
    (must do)

sellam karanava: → **sellam kala yuthui** *or*
                    sellam karanna/karanda/karannata o:na
    (must play)

call karanava: → **call kala yuthui** *or*
                    call karanna/karannata/karanda o:na
    (must call)

kanava: → **kae: yuthui** *or*
                    kanna/kannata/kanda o:na
    (must eat)

bonava: → **biya yuthui** or
bonna/bonda/bonnata o:na
(must drink)

yanava: → **ya: yuthui** or
yanna/yanda/yannata o:na
(must go)

enava: → **a: yuthui** or
enna/enda/ennata o:na
(must come)

kiyanava: → **kiva/kiya yuthui** or
kiyanna/kiyanda/kiyannata o:na
(must tell)

uyanava: → **iviya yuthui** or
uyanna/uyanda/uyannata o:na
(must cook)

nidhiyanava: → **nidhiya yuthui** or
nidhayanna/nidhiyannata/nidhiyanda o:na
(must sleep)

gannava: → **gatha yuthui** or
ganna/ganda/gannata o:na
(must take)

thiyenava: → **thibiya yuthui** or
thibenna/thibennata/thibenda o:na
(must have/be there)

Now let us see how to make sentences.

Eya: heta potha kiyaviya yuthui.
Eya: heta potha kiyavanna o:na.
(He/She must read the book tomorrow.)

Mama e:ka balanna o:na.
Mama e:ka baeliya yuthui.
(I should see/look at it.)

Oya: adha bath uyanna o:na.
Oya adha bath iviya yuthui.
(You ought to cook rice today.)

Gaha kaepiya yuthui.
Gaha kapanna o:na.
(The tree should be cut.)

Eya: potha kiyavamin/kiyava kiyava sitiya yuthui.
Eya: potha kiyavamin/kiyava kiyava sitinna o:na.
(She/He must be reading the book.)

In both ordinary and continuous perfect tenses, there is another popular method which is optional. Here, you put "***thibuna:***" at the end of the perfect tense verb, and the verb itself is changed to the infinitive. Optionally, you may append "**-ta**" to the doer.

Mama e:ka balala: thibiya yuthui.
Mama e:ka balala: thiyenna o:na.
Mama/Mata e:ka balanna thibuna: . (When you suffix
"-ta" to "mama", it becomes "**mata**")
(I should have seen it.)

Eya: liyumak liya: thibiya yuthui.
Eya: liyumak liya: thiyenna o:na.
Eya:/Eya:ta liyumak liyanna thibuna: .
(He/She should have written a letter.)

Lamaya: sellam karamin/kara kara sitiya yuthui.
Lamaya: sellam karamin/kara kara sitinna/inna o:na.
Lamaya:/Lamaya:ta sellam karamin/kara kara
inna/sitinna thibuna: .
(The child should have been playing.)

Gaha kapamin/kapa kapa sitiya yuthui.
Gaha kapamin/kapa kapa inna/sitinna o:na.
(The tree must be being cut.)

Gaha kapala: thibiya yuthui.
Gaha kapala: thiyenna o:na.
Gaha kapanna thibuna: . (Here "*gaha*" is not the doer,
but the object; so "-ta" cannot be suffixed)
(The tree should have been cut.)

Mama lassanai. → **mama lassana viya yuthui.**
                → **mama lassana venna o:na.**
(I should be/become beautiful.)

Eya: kri:dakayek. → **eya: kri:dakayek viya yuthui.**
                 → **eya: kri:dakayek venna o:na.**

(He should be/become a sportsman.)

Api bus eke: . → **api bus eke: viya yuthui.**

→ **api bus eke: venna o:na.**

→ **api bus eke: inna o:na.** (This form can only be used with "*o:na*")

(We should be in the bus.)

You can easily form the other variants of this sentence pattern. To form the positive question, append "-dha" at the end of the helping verb ("*yuthuidha*" is often simplified to "***yuthudha***").

To make the negative statement, put "naehae" after the helping verb ("*yuthui*" becomes "**yuthu**" here). To make the negative question, put "*naedhdha*" after the helping verb. In fact, you already knew those methods. Right?

Eya: potha kiyaviya yuthuidha/yuthudha?
Eya: potha kiyavanna o:nadha?
(Should he/she read the book?)

Eya: potha kiyaviya yuthu naehae.
Eya: potha kiyavanna o:na naehae.
(He/She should not read the book.)

Eya: potha kiyaviya yuthu naedhdha?
Eya: potha kiyavanna o:na naedhdha?
(Should he/she not read the book?)

Eya: potha kiyaviya yuthui ne:dha?
Eya: potha kiyavanna o:na ne:dha?
(He/She should read the book. Shouldn't he/she?)

Eya: potha kiyaviya yuthu naehae ne:dha?
Eya: potha kiyavanna o:na naehae ne:dha?
(He/She should not read the book. Shouldn't he?)

Gaha kapamin/kapa kapa thibiya yuthudha?
Gaha kapamin/kapa kapa thiyenna o:nadha?
(Should the tree be being cut?)

Gaha kapala: thibiya yuthu naehae.
Gaha kapala: thiyenna o:na naehae.
(The tree should not have been cut.)

2. puluvan / hakiy

– can

Here too you put *"puluvan"* after the tense verb. The tense verb takes the infinitive form. Moreover, you should append "**-ta**" to the doer.

Sherinta lassanata natanna puluvan.
(Sherin can dance beautifully.)

Sherinta lassanata natamin/nata nata inna puluvan.
(Sherin can be dancing beautifully.)

Eya:ta lassana venna puluvan.

(She/He can be/become beautiful.)

Apita pilotla: venna puluvan.

(We can be/become pilots.)

Mata panthiye: inna puluvan.

(I can be in the class.)

(With prepositional part, you have to use *"inna"* only.)

To make the negative statement, just replace *"puluvan"* with *"baehae"*.

To make the positive question, append "-dha" to *"puluvan"*. And to make the negative question, append "-dha" to *"baehae"* (and often *"baehaedha"* is simplified to *"baeridha"*).

Sherinta natanna baehae.

(Sherin cannot dance.)

Sherinta natanna puluvandha?

(Can Sherin dance?)

Sherinta natanna baridha?

(Can Sherin not dance?)

Sherinta natanna puluvan ne:dha?

(Sherin can dance. Can't she?)

Sherinta natanna baehae ne:dha?

(Sherin cannot dance. Can she?)

3.puluvan vuna:

- could (was able to)

You do the same changes to the tense verb as you did in
"puluvan" (can).

> **Dorista lassanata natanna puluvan una: .**
> (Doris could dance beautifully.)

> **Dorista lassanata natanna baeri una: .**
> (Doris could not dance beautifully.)

> **Dorista lassanata natanna puluvan una:dha?**
> (Could Doris dance beautifully?)

> **Dorista lassanata natanna baeri una:dha?**
> (Could Doris not dance beautifully?)

> **Dorista lassanata natanna puluvan una: ne:dha?**
> (Doris could dance beautifully. Couldn't she?)

> **Dorista lassanata natanna baeri una: ne:dha?** (Doris
> could not dance beautifully. Could she?)

> **Dorista natamin/nata nata inna puluvan una: .**
> (Doris could/was able to be dancing.)

> **Eya:ta e:ka ivara karala: thiyanna puluvan una: .**
> (He/She could/was able to have finished it.)

> **Gahak kapanna puluvan una: .**
> (A tree could be cut.)

Sherinta lassana venna puluvan una: .

(Sherin could/was able to be/become beautiful.)

Apita pilotla: venna puluvan una: .

(We could/was able to be/become pilots.)

Mata panthiye: inna puluvan una: .

(I could/was able to be in the class.)

You can make the future time sentence of "*puluvan*" (can/be able to) with "***puluvan ve:vi***" (will be able to). As you can remember "*ve:vi*" is the future time form of "*venava:*".

Dorista lassanata natanna puluvan ve:vi.

(Doris will be able to dance beautifully.)

Dorista lassanata natanna baeri ve:vi.

(Doris will not be able to dance beautifully.)

Dorista lassanata natanna puluvan ve:vidha?

(Will Doris be able to dance beautifully?)

Dorista lassanata natanna baeri ve:vidha?

(Will Doris not be able to dance beautifully?)

Dorista lassanata natanna puluvan ve:vi ne:dha?

(Doris will be able to dance beautifully. Won't she?)

Dorista lassanata natanna baeri ve:vi ne:dha?

(Doris will not be able to dance beautifully. Will she?)

Dorista natamin/nata nata inna puluvan ve:vi.

(Doris will be able to be dancing.)

Eya:ta e:ka ivara karala: thiyanna puluvan ve:vi.
(He/She will be able to have finished it.)

Gahak kapanna puluvan ve:vi.
(A tree will be able to be cut.)

Sherinta lassana venna puluvan ve:vi.
(Sherin will be able to be/become beautiful.)
Apita pilotla: venna puluvan ve:vi.
(We will be able to be/become pilots.)

Mata panthiye: inna puluvan ve:vi.
(I will be able to be in the class.)

4. avashyai, o:na, o:ne

– need , want to

You take the tense verb and put one of above helping verbs after
it. The doer is appended with "**-ta**" suffix too. You can make the
variants as usual now.

Mata natanna o:na/o:ne/avashyai.
(I need dance.)

Mata natanna o:na/o:ne/avashya naehae.
(I need not dance.)

Mata natanna o:nadha/o:nedha/avashyadha?
(Need I dance?)

Mata natanna o:na/o:ne/avashya naedhdha?
(Need I not dance?)

Mata dhaksha venna o:na/o:ne/avashyai.
(I need/want to be clever.)

Eya:ta doctor kenek venna: o:na/o:ne/avashyai.
(He/She need/wants to be a doctor.)

Apita ethaena inna o:na/o:ne/avashyai.
(We need/want to be there.)

You can make the past time form of this helping verb with
"o:na una" or *"o:ne una"* or *"avashya vuna:"*. The future time
form can be constructed with *"o:na/o:ne/avashya ve:vi"*.

Mata natanna o:na/o:ne/avashya vuna: .
(I wanted to dance.)

Mata natanna o:na/o:ne/avashya vune: naehae.
(I did not want to dance.)

Mata natanna o:na/o:ne/avashya vuna:dha?
(Did I want to dance?)

Mata natanna o:na/o:ne/avashya vune: naedhdha?
(Did I not want to dance?)

Mata natanna o:na/o:ne/avashya ve:vi.
(I will want to dance.)

Mata natanna o:na/o:ne/avashya vena ekak naehae.
(I will not want to dance.)

Mata natanna o:na/o:ne/avashya ve:vidha?
(Will I want to dance?)

**Mata natanna o:na/o:ne/avashya vena ekak
naedhdha?**
(Will I not want to dance?)

5. aethi, venna/venda/vennata puluvan
– may/might

You just have to put this after the tense verb. When making the
negative statement, you can put *"venna baehae"* or *"naethiva
aethi"*.

And if you use *"naethiva aethi"*, then the tense verb must be in
"-nne:" form.

Teacher uganvanava: aethi.
Teacher uganvanava: venna puluvan.
(The female teacher might teach.)

Teacher uganvanava: venna baehae.
Teacher uganvanne: naethiva aethi.
(The female teacher may not teach.)

Teacher uganvanava: aethidha?
Teacher uganvanava: venna puluvandha?
(May the female teacher teach?)

Teacher uganvanava: venna baeridha?
Teacher uganvanne: naethiva aethidha?
(May the female teacher not teach?)

Amma: bath uyamin/uya uya aethi.
Amma: bath uyamin/uya uya innava: aethi.
Amma: bath uyamin/uya uya innava: venna puluvan.
(The mother may be cooking rice.)

Amma: bath uyamin/uya uya naethiva aethi.
Amma: bath uyamin/uya uya inne: naethiva aethi.
Amma: bath uyamin/uya uya innava: venna baehae.
(The mother may not be cooking rice.)

Amma: bath uyamin/uya uya aethidha?
Amma: bath uyamin/uya uya innava: aethidha?
Amma: bath uyamin/uya uya innava: venna
puluvandha?
(May the mother be cooking rice?)

Eya: e:ka karala: aethi.
Eya: e:ka karala venna puluvan.
(He/She may have done it.)

Eya: e:ka karala: naethiva aethi.
Eya: e:ka karala: venna baehae.
(He/She may not have done it.)

Eya: e:ka karala: aethidha?
Eya: e:ka karala: venna puluvandha?
(May he/she have done it?)

Eya: nurse kenek venna aethi/puluvan.
(He may be a nurse.)

Rita lassana venna aethi/puluvan.
(Rita may be beautiful.)
Lamai pittaniye: venna aethi/puluvan.
(Children may be in the ground.)

6. thiyenava:, sidhdha venava:, sidhu venava:

- have to

The verb is changed to infinitive form, and you append "-ta" to the doer.

Kellyta market ekata yanna thiyenava: .
Kellyta market ekata yanna sidhdha/sidhu venava: .
(Kelly has to go the market.)

Kellyta market ekata yanna naehae. ("thiyenava:" part
is dropped.)
**Kellyta market ekata yanna sidhdha/sidhu venne:
naehae.**
(Kelly has not to go the market.)

Kellyta market ekata yanna thiyenava:dha?
Kellyta market ekata yanna sidhdha/sidhu
venava:dha?
(Has Kelly to go to the market?)

Kellyta market ekata yanna naedhdha?
Kellyta market ekata yanna sidhdha/sidhu venne:
naedhdha?
(Has Kelly not to go the market?)

Gaha kapanna thiyenava: .
Gaha kapanna sidhdha/sidhu venava: .
(The tree has to be cut.)

Mata engineer kenek venna thiyenava: .
Mata engineer kenek venna sidhdha/sidhu venava: .
(I have to be/become an engineer.)

Eya:ta potha kiyavamin/kiyava kiyava inna
thiyenava: .
Eya:ta potha kiyavamin/kiyava kiyava inna
sidhdha/sidhu venava: .
(He/She has to be reading the book.)

You can make the past time of it with "*thibuna:*" or "*vuna:*" or
"*sidhdha/sidhu vuna:*" and future time with "*thiye:vi*" or "*ve:vi*"
or "*sidhdha/sidhu ve:vi*".

Kellyta market ekata yanna thibuna:/vuna: .
Kellyta market ekata yanna sidhdha/sidhu vuna: .
(Kelly had to go to the market.)

Kellyta market ekata yanna thiye:vi/ve:vi.
Kellyta market ekata yanna sidhdha/sidhu ve:vi.
(Kelly will have to go to the market.)

Technically, Sinhala has no helping verbs on their own; but as you just learned, you can easily match some Sinhala patterns with the English helping verbs. This is just a trick I used to teach Sinhala quickly.

In fact, what we have done is to connect two verbs together to give some composite meaning, as we do in English like "*be going to + eat*", "*want to + go*", "*plan to + come*", etc.

There are some popular Sinhala patterns (but they do not necessarily correspond to English helping verbs), and I will show some of them below. With the rules that you have learned so far, you can make all the variants of them.

The keyword that you must pay attention is underlined. In some cases, the doer must be suffixed "-ta" (Carefully remember those points in the given examples below). Special points (if any) are made in short after the sentence pattern. There is nothing new to learn now; only the pattern is pointed out in particular.

Mama paththaraya kiyavanna
yanava:/yanne:/hadhanne: .
(I am going/about to read the newspaper.)

Baba: a'ndanna yanne:/yanava:/hadhanne: .
(The baby is going/about to cry.)

Api pitath venna yanne:/yanava:/hadhanne: .
(We are going/about to leave.)

Mama kiyavanna neme: yanne:/hadhanne: .
(I am not going/about to read.)

Baba: a'ndanna neme: yanne:/hadhanne: .
(The baby is not going/about to cry.)

Api pitath venna neme yanne:/hadhanne: .
(We are not going/about to leave.)

Mama kiyavannadha yanne:/hadhanne:?
(Am I going/about to read?)

Baba: a'ndannadha yanne:/hadhanne:?
(Is the baby going/about to cry?)

Mama kiyavanna neme:dha yanne:/hadhanne:?
(Am I not going/about to read?)

Baba: a'ndanna neme:dha yanne:/hadhanne:?
(Is the baby not going/about to cry?)

Above is the English pattern "is about to" or "is going to".
Below is its past time pattern "was about to" or "was going to".

Mama paththaraya kiyavanna giye:/hadhuve: .
(I was going/about to read the newspaper.)

Baba: a'ndanna giye:/hadhuve: .
(The baby was going/about to cry.)

Api pitath venna giye:/hadhuve: .
(We were going/about to leave.)

Mama kiyavanna neme: giye:/hadhuve: .
(I was not going/about to read.)

Baba: a'ndanna neme: giye:/hadhuve: .
(The baby was not going/about to cry.)

Mama kiyavannadha giye:/hadhuve:?
(Was I going/about to read?)

Baba: a'ndannadha giye:/hadhuve:?
(Was the baby going/about to cry?)

Mama kiyavanna neme:dha giye:/hadhuve:?
(Was I not going/about to read?)

Baba: a'ndanna neme:dha giye:/hadhuve:?
(Was the baby not going/about to cry?)

**Mama labana sathiye: viba:gaya karanna
hitha:gena/hithan innava: .**
Mama labana sathiye: viba:gaya karanna <u>hithanava:</u> .
(I <u>am planning to</u> do the exam next week.)

Eya: heta e:ka kiyanna hitha:gena/hithan naehae.
(He is not planning to tell it tomorrow.)

Above is the "is planning to" pattern.

Joshta udhe: na:la: <u>purudhui</u>.

(Josh <u>is used to</u> bathe in the morning.)

Mata pa:n ka:la: purudhu naehae.

(I am not used to eat bread.)

Above, the English keyword is "is used to", not the helping verb "used to" (there is a difference between "used to" and "be used to"). Also, the Sinhala verb should be in "-la:" form (the kind of verb form that you use in perfect tense). The "used to" pattern is shown below.

Mama e: dhavasvala havasata sellam karanna <u>purudhuva hitiya:</u> .

(I <u>used to</u> play in the afternoon those days.)

Eya: cigarette bonna purudhuva hitiye: naehae.

(He used not to smoke.)

Mama Sinhala igena ganna <u>a:sai</u>.

(I <u>like/love</u> to learn Sinhala.)

Eya: uyanna a:sa naehae.

(He does not like to cook.)

Gerunds (Verbal Nouns) in Sinhala

We learned how to derive two forms of adjectives from a verb.
You can derive a noun (a gerund) from a verb too. Let us learn
how to do that. There are two methods here.

1. You change remove "va:" from a "-nava:" verb and put "*eka*"
after that. This method is uniform and easy to make.

> *karanava:* → **karana eka** *(doing, to do)*
> *sellam karanava:* → **sellam karana eka** *(playing, to play)*
> *call karanava:* → **call karana eka** *(calling, to call)*
> *balanava:* → **balana eka** *(looking/watching, to look/to
> watch)*
> *kanava:* → **kana eka** *(eating, to eat)*
> *bonava:* → **bona eka** *(drinking, to drink)*
> *innava:* → **inna eka** *(being)*
> *sitinava:* → **sitina eka** *(being, staying)*

2. You remove "Xnava:" part from the verb, and suffix "-**i:ma**"
or "-**ae:ma**" to it. In addition, the first syllable of the verb is
modified. If the first syllable rhymes like "X<u>a</u>", it is often
changed to "X<u>ae</u>"; try to understand how the first syllable
changes by studying those words. There are some exceptions too.

> *balanava:* → **baeli:ma** *(looking/watching)*
> *thalanava:* → **thaeli:ma** *(beating)*
> *natanava:* → **naeti:ma** *(dancing)*
>
> *uyanava:* → *(iyi:ma→)* **ivi:ma** *(cooking)*
> *pupuranava:* → **pipiri:ma** *(blasting, exploding)*

karanava: → **kiri:ma** (doing)

sellam karanava: → **sellam kiri:ma** (playing)

call karanava: → **call kiri:ma** (calling)

thiyenava:/thibenava: → **thibi:ma** (having)

kanava: → **kae:ma** (eating)

bonava: → **bi:ma** (drinking)

yanava: → **yae:ma** (going)

naliyanava: → **naliyae:ma** (squirming)

enava: → **e:ma** (coming)

dhenava: → **dhi:ma** (giving)

gannava: → **gaeni:ma** (taking)

venava: → **vi:ma** (being, becoming, happening)

loku venava: → **loku vi:ma** (growing, becoming large)

innava: → **i'ndhi:ma** (being)

sitinava: → **siti:ma** (being, staying)

You can construct this verbal noun with other tense verbs too. You use a similar method as described above.

Kanava:

→ **kamin/kaka: i'ndhi:ma/siti:ma**

→ **kamin/kaka: inna eka**

 (being eating, to be eating)

karanava:

→ **karamin/kara kara i'ndhi:ma/siti:ma**

→ **karamin/kara kara inna eka**

 (being doing, to be doing)

Kanava:
→ *ka:la: thibi:ma*
→ *ka:la: thiyena eka*
 (having eaten, to have eaten)

Karanava:
→ *karala: thibi:ma*
→ *karala: thiyena eka*
(having done, to have done)

You can also form the verbal noun that has the opposite meaning too. You just have to prefix "**no-**" (this prefix is similar to "*un-/dis-*" prefix in English) to the verbal noun that you constructed above. When the verbal noun consists of several parts, then you have to put this "no-" to the last part.

Kiri:ma → **nokiri:ma** *(not doing)*
karana eka → **nokarana eka** *(not doing)*

Kae:ma → **nokae:ma** *(not eating)*
kana eka → **nokana eka** *(not eating)*

bi:ma → **nobi:ma** *(not drinking)*
bona eka → **nobona eka** *(not drinking)*

sellam kiri:ma → **sellam nokiri:ma** *(not playing)*
sellam karana eka → **sellam nokarana eka** *(not playing)*

call kiri:ma → **call nokiri:ma** *(not calling)*
call karana eka → **call nokarana eka** *(not calling)*

loku vi:ma → **loku novi:ma** *(not growing)*
loku vena eka → **loku novena eka** *(not growing)*

natamin/nata nata i'ndhi:ma → **natamin/nata nata noim'di:ma** *(not being dancing)*

natamin/nata nata inna eka → **natamin/nata nata noinna eka** *(not being dancing)*

natala: thibi:ma → **natala: nothibi:ma** *(not having danced)*

natala: thiyena eka → **natala: nothiyena eka** *(not having danced)*

You now know that a verb (in its any form, even in the gerund form) has the right to have an object (if possible), adverbs, and prepositional parts. Therefore, here in the gerund too, you can include one or several/all of them. You know that in Sinhala you put these (complementary) words before the verb form as follows.

Film ekak baeli:ma/balana eka *(watching a film)*

Film ekak nobaeli:ma/nobalana eka *(not watching a film)*

Gahak kaepi:ma/kapana eka *(cutting a tree)*

Lassanata livi:ma/liyana eka *(writing beautifully)*

Ikamin yae:ma/yana eka *(going quickly)*

Gedharata e:ma/ena eka *(coming to the house)*

Gahak ikmanin kaepi:ma/kapana eka *(cutting a tree quickly)*

Udhe: bath kae:ma/kana eka *(eating rice in the morning)*

> ***Ya:luvan ekka sathutin bath kae:ma/kana eka*** *(eating rice happily with friends)*

You can use gerunds as you use normal nouns in the sentence.

Kiyavi:ma minisa: sampu:rna karanava:.
(Reading makes a man perfect.)

Daeki:ma visva:sa kiri:mayi.
(Seeing is believing.)

Viba:gaye:dhi sindhu ki:ma/kiyana eka ho'ndha naehae.
(Singing in the exam is not good.)

Mama udhe: TV bala bala inna ekata a:sa naehae.
(I do not like watching TV in the morning.)

Mama aeththa nokiyana ekata a:sa naehae.
(I do not like not telling the truth.)

Note:

In English, after the verbs such as love, like, give, hate do not have "to" when there is a noun, but have "to" when there is a verb (that is, infinitive verb form). For example,

I like tea.

I like to read.

However, in Sinhala for both cases, you put "-ta" (equivalent to English "to"). And you know there are three possible forms of Sinhala infinitive form too. For example,

> **Mama mala_ta_ kamathiy.**
> (I like the flower.)
>
> **Mama kiyavanna_ta_/kanna/kanda kamathiy.**
> (I like to read.)

Note:

There are some special verbs that don't end with "-nava:". Actually, you can convert these verbs into the usual "-nava:" form too. Let us see those verbs most popular among native speakers. These verbs end with "-yi". To make the negative statement, you remove the "-yi" suffix and put "naehae" after that. To make the positive question, append "-dha" to the verb. To make the negative question, remove "-yi" and put "naedhdha" after the verb.

> *A:dhareyi* (love) ("nava:" form is "a:dharaya karanava:")

Kaemathiyi, a:sai *(like) ("kaemathi venava:", "a:sa karanava:")*

Akamaethiyi *(don't like, dislike) ("akamaethi venava:")*

Apriyayi *(hate/abhor) ("apriya karanava:")*

Bayayi *(is afraid to/of) ("baya venava:")*

Let us see how to make sentences with these verb forms.

Mama oya:ta a:dhareyi.
(I love you.)

Mama oya:ta a:dhare naehae.
(I do not love you.)

Mama oya:ta a:dhareyidha?
(Do I love you?)

Mama oya:ta a:dhare naedhdha?
(Do I not love you?)

Mama ballanta kaemathiyi.
(I like dogs.)

Mama ballanta kaemathi naehae.
(I do not like dogs.)

Mama ballanta kaemathiyidha?
(Do I like dogs?)

Mama ballanta kaemathi naedhdha?
(Do I not like dogs?)

Comparative Adjectives and Adverbs

Sinhala has equivalent adverbs to "very" or "so". That is "*itha:*" or "*boho:*" or "*godak*" (this adverb is popular but should be minimally used). You put one of these adverbs in front of the adjective or adverb.

Eya: boho:/itha:/godak lassanai.
(She/He is very beautiful.)

Peter boho:/itha:/godak loku pothak kiyavanava: .
(Peter reads a very big book.)

Ya:luva: boho:/itha:/godak lassanata liyanava: .
(The friend writes very beautifully.)

These same adverbs make Sinhala adjectives and adverbs comparative too. Optionally there is another adverb "*vada:*" for this.

Boho:/itha:/godak/vada: lassana (more beautiful)
boho:/itha:/godak/vada: loku (larger)
boho:/itha:/godak/vada: lassanata (more beautifully)
boho:/itha:/godak/vada: lokuvata (more largely)

Let us make a few sentences with comparative adjectives and adverbs.

Mama vada: loku potha gannam.
(I shall take the larger book.)

Eya vada: ikmanin kanava: .
(He/She eats more quickly.)

Sherin vada: lassanai.
(Sherin is more beautiful.)

Optionally you can put another noun to compare with (as in *"than somebody/something"* in English). In Sinhala, you just put the other noun before the *"vada:"*(you may change *"vada:"* to *"vaediya"* too). Here *"vada:"* part has two functions – one is to denote "more", and the other is to function as "than". In addition, "-ta" suffix is appended to this additional noun.

Sherin Ritata vada:/vaediya lassanai.
(Sherin is more beautiful than Rita.)

Shane Johnta vada:/vaediya ikmanin liyanava:.
(Shane writes more quickly than John.)

Superlative

To make an adjective or an adverb superlative, you just append "**-ma**" suffix to it.

*Lassana → **lassanama** (the most beautiful)*
*loku → **lokuma** (the biggest)*
*ikmanin → **ikmaninma** (the most quickly)*

Now let us make a few sentences with superlative adjectives and adverbs.

Sherin panthiye: lassanama lamaya: .
(Sherin is the most beautiful child in the class.)

Eya: lokuma potha gaththa: .
(He took the biggest book.)

Emphasizing

This same "-ma" is used in Sinhala to emphasize (or make the meaning stronger) words just as it did to adjectives and adverbs as shown above. Specially, this technique is used with prepositions (and with conjunctions, as you will learn in a moment) as well. In English, therefore, it is somewhat similar to "*just*" (to emphasize).

> *Uda* → **udama** *(just on)*
> *yata* → **yatama** *(just under)*
> *sa'ndhaha* → **sa'ndhahama** *(just for)*
> *thulin* → **thulinma** *(just through)*

Let us see a few examples using these.

> **Potha me:saya udama thiyanna.**
> (Put the book just on the table.)

> **Api ka:maraya athule:ma innava: .**
> (We stay just inside/in the room.)

You can append this same "-ma" suffix to a noun. Then it makes the noun reflexive as follows.

> *Mama* → **mamama/manma** *(I myself)*
> *Api* → **apima** *(we ourselves)*
> *Eya:* → **eya:ma** *(she herself or he himself)*
> *oya:* → **oya:ma** *(you yourself)*
> *oya:la:* → **oya:la:ma** *(you yourselves)*
> *u:* → **u:ma** *(it itself – with animals)*
> *e:ka* → **e:kama** *(it itself – with inanimate things)*
> *un* → **unma** *(they themselves – with animals)*

> *e:va: → **e:va:ma** (they themselves – with inanimate things)*
> *John → **Johnma** (John himself)*
> *lamaya: → **lamaya:ma** (the child himself/herself)*

We will see a several examples.

> **Mamama e:ka karannam.**
> (I myself shall do it.)

> **Eya:ma sellam karanna o:na.**
> (He himself/She herself must play.)

You know some Sinhala prepositions are suffixed to the noun itself. In that case, you append "-ma" even after that prepositional suffix.

> **Eya: <u>magenma</u> e:ka ahanava: .**
> (He asks it <u>from me myself</u>.)

> **Oya: gedharatama yanna o:na.**
> (You must go to the house itself.)

You can append "-ma" to a tense verb too; but now it is slightly modified to "**-mayi**". As in all the above cases, the action denoted by the verb is emphasized ("definitely/of course"). However, because "definitely" part is not included as an adverb in the original Sinhala sentence, I have struck it out.

> **Mama e:ka karanava:mayi.**
> (I will do it ~~definitely~~.)

> **Eya: kivva:mayi.**
> (He said it ~~definitely~~.)

Lamaya: potha kiyavamin/kiyava kiyava innavamayi.
(The child is ~~definitely~~ reading the book.)

Amma: e:ka kiyala: thiyenava:mayi.
(The mother has ~~definitely~~ said it.)

Optionally you may append "**-va**" suffix to the object (the object must be a living/animate thing). Actually native speakers use that so often. When you append it to "*mama*", it becomes "*ma:va*".

Mama oya:/oya:va daekka:.
(I saw you.)

Oya: ma:va/mama dhannavadha?
(Do you know me?)

Eya: sherinva/Sherin dhanne: naedhdha?
(Does she/he not know Sherin?)

Kavudha balla:va/balla: maeruve:?
(Who killed the dog?)

"thamai"

In Sinhala, there is an interesting way of expression that you cannot find in English directly. For that a special word "**thamai**" or "**thama:**" is used, and it makes the word it is used with stronger/emphasized. There is no negative statement or negative question forms for this pattern, and instead use the normal sentence pattern for that.

Actually, depending on the way the sentence is pronounced, it may convey a formidable/threatening kind of meaning or a lenient/naïve/agreeing kind of meaning (So, practice listening to both ways of pronunciation to get the feeling). Because this usage is very popular among native speakers, I will describe it in detail in four sections.

1. You can put this word after a noun in the sentence. In English, you can use the pattern "*It is <somebody/something> who/that/which <...>*" for this. The verb must be in the "-nne:" form (for the present time), and "-ve:" form (for the past time). To make the context clearer, I have used additional English expression (struck through) in the first example to let you feel the real meaning of the Sinhala sentence.

> **Mama thamai e:ka karanne: .**
> (It is me who does it. ~~So what?~~) (threatening)
> (~~Well~~, it is me who does it.) (naïve)
>
> **Mama thamaidha e:ka karanne: ?**
> (Is it me who does it?)
>
> **Bill thamai boru kiyanne: .**
> (It's Bill who lies.)
>
> **Bill thamaidha boru kiyanne: ?**
> (Is it Bill who lies?)

The above two examples emphasize the subject of the sentence. You can emphasize the object of the sentence as in the following examples. In this case, to make it clearer, you would better use the object with "-va" suffix.

Man Rita/Ritava thamai i:ye daekke: .
(It is/was Rita that I saw yesterday. ~~Who dare deny it?~~)
(threatening)
(~~Well~~, it is/was Rita that I saw yesterday.) (naïve)

Man Ritava thamaidha i:ye daekke: ?
(Is/Was it Rita that I saw yesterday?)

E: ballava thamai maeruve: .
(It was/is that dog that was killed.)

E: ballava thamaidha maeruve: ?
(Was/Is that dog that was killed?)

2. You can put it after a tense verb. To make the context clearer, I have used additional English expression (struck through) in the first example to let you feel the real meaning of the Sinhala sentence.

Mama eya:va dhannava: thamai.
(I know him/her. ~~So what?~~) (threatening)
(~~Well~~, I know him/her.) (naïve)

Eya: e:ka kala: thamai.
(She/He did it.)

Mama sindhu kiyala thiyenava: thamai.
(I have sung.)

Api sellam karamin/kara kara hitiya: thamai.
(We were playing.)

3. You can put it after a preposition too (giving the same two meanings as described in the two above sections (threatening or naïve). The verb takes the "-nne:" or "-ve:" form.

Mama me:saya uda thamai hi'ndha ganne: .
(I am sitting on the table. ~~So what?~~) (threatening)
(~~Well,~~ I am sitting on the table.) (naïve)

Api ahasa yata thamai inne: .
(We are under the sky.)

4. This style is so interesting and popular. Always used with phrases (phrases are a set of words, but not a complete sentence) - most probably just with a single word (verb, noun, adjective, adverb, or preposition). This usage has the same two meanings (threatening, or naïve), and additionally it conveys an ironic meaning. Let us see a few examples of this usage within a simple context (I will write the sentence showing the context in English). Without knowing the context, you cannot understand it properly because there is no complete sentence here.

<u>With a noun:</u>

"Are you sure you met Mr. John?"
Ow, Ow… **John thamai**.
(yeah, yeah… I told you thousand times… It is John that I met.) (kind of nagging/naive)

"Who stole the pen?"
John thamai.
(It was John. Who else?) (threatening)

"Who ate my piece of cake?"
hahaha… **John thamai.**
(John ate. Hahaha) (usually you say it as a joke and with a laughter, and everybody knows that John did not eat it; it's ironic)

With a verb:

"Did you go to see the girlfriend, Son?"
ow, ow… **giya: thamai.**
(yeah, yeah… I went.) (kind of nagging)

"Did you go to see her even after I have told you not to go?"
ow… **giya: thamai.**
(yes, I went. You can't stop me.) (threatening)

"Hey Son, did you really go to see your aunt? I told you yesterday to go there."
haha… **giya: thamai.**
(I went. Hahaha) (really he has not gone.)

With an adjective:

"She is really a beautiful girl."

lassanai thamai.
(yeah, really she is beautiful.) (agreeing and naïve)

"Who says you are smart?"
smart thamai.
(why not? I am certainly smart.) (threatening)

"His boyfriend is handsome."
hahaha... **handsome thamai.**
(hahaha... he is handsome.) (ironic and it really says "no
he is not")

Sometimes, when you want to convey this ironic meaning with
an adjective or adverb, you can simply say "**bambuva thamai**"
or "**redhdha thamai**".

"His boyfriend is handsome."
hahaha... **bambuva/redhdha thamai.**

So far, what we have learned is to construct a Sinhala sentence.
We learned to make different kinds of simple sentences, wh
questions in all tenses (ordinary, continual, perfect, perfect
continuous), in all three times (present, past, future), in all six
variants (positive and negative statements, positive and negative
questions, positive and negative tag questions), using helping
verbs, adjectives, adverbs, prepositional parts, etc.

Joining Sinhala Sentences Together

Usually we join several sentences into one larger/longer sentence too. In English we do this in a few ways, and the two most popular ways are firstly using conjunctions like "because", "though", "if", etc (called "**complex sentences**"), and secondly using the conjunctions of "and", "but", "or" (called "**compound sentences**").

First I will talk about constructing complex sentences (long sentences that use such conjunctions as "because", "if", etc). Here, there must be (at least) two sentences, and one of them is the main **sentence/clause**. The other sentence that may be called "subordinate clause" is kind of "causal" (that is, the subordinate clause says/has some reason on which the main clause (main action) is dependent). Let us examine this in English first.

Because I studied hard, I could pass the exam.

In this complex sentence, "I could pass the exam" is the main clause (because it is primarily what we wanted to convey to others), and "I studied hard" is the subordinate clause (as you can notice, the main clause happened because of the action this sentence has). "*because*" which is placed just before the subordinate clause is the conjunction.

However, in Sinhala, the conjunction is placed just after the subordinate clause (while doing so, sometimes the verb form of the subordinate clause is modified).

Let us learn about Sinhala conjunctions one by one.

1. Nisa: , Hindha:

- because/as/since

First I write the two clauses separately as follows, and then show you how to join them.

Mama mahansiyen pa:dam kala: . (I studied hard.)
Mata viba:gaya pass venna puluvan vuna: . (I could pass the exam.)

Now let us use *"nisa:"* or *"hindha"* to join these sentences. You already construct this kind of sentences in English, and therefore it is not a problem at all to identify the subordinate clause (trust on your English language skill, and Sinhala follows almost the same rules here).

Here, *"mama mahansiyen pa:dam <u>kala:</u>"* (I studied hard) is the subordinate clause. Therefore, you just put the conjunction after that, and simply write the other sentence thereafter.

> **Mama mahansiyen pa:dam <u>kala</u> nisa:/hindha: mata viba:gaya pass venna puluvan vuna: .**
> (Because I studied hard, I could pass the exam.)

However, the verb form in the subordinate clause has changed a bit. It is a very simple modification. Apply the following rules. You must follow these same rules in most of other conjunctions too.

(a) If the verb is in past time (like, "*kala:*", "*baenna:*", "*vuna:*"),
then the last/ending long vowel is just made a short vowel.

> *kala:* → **kala**
> *baenna:* → **baenna**
> *vuna:* → **vuna**
> *maeruva:* → **maeruva**

Or else, there is another alternative too, and that is to change the
verb into "-pu" verb form (you learned how to construct this
verb form earlier when we talked about deriving an adjective out
of a verb).

I think it is easier and methodical if you derive the "-pu" verb
form from the present tense (original) verb, rather than from its
past tense verb (because when we construct the past tense form
from the present tense verb itself, it is already deformed).
However, some verbs may not possess this "-pu" form.

> *kala:* → **karapu**
> *baenna:* → **baenapu**
> *maeruva:* → **marapu**
> *vuna:* → **vunu** *(why this form? If you can't remember,*
> *read the past lessons again)*
>
> **Mama mahansiyen pa:dam <u>karapu</u> nisa:/hindha:**
> **mata viba:gaya pass venna puluvan vuna: .**
> (Because I studied hard, I could pass the exam.)

(b) If the verb is in present time (like, "*karanava:*", "*baninava:*",
"*venava:*"), then the ending "va:" part is removed.

*karanava: → **karana***
*baninava: → **banina***
*venava: → **vena***
*maranava: → **marana***

Lamayi sellam karanava: . (Children play.)
Egollo thuva:la venava: . (They get injured.)

Lamai sellam <u>karana</u> hindha: egollo thuva:la venava: .
(Because children play, they are injured.)

Mama mahansiyen pa:dam <u>karana</u> nisa:/hindha: mata viba:gaya pass venna puluvan.
(Because I study hard, I can pass the exam.)

(c) If the verb is in negative form (like, "*karanne: naehae*" or "*kale: naehae*"), then the "*naehae*" part is changed to "***naethi***".

*karanne: naehae → **karanne: naethi***
*kale: naehae → **kale: naethi***

Lamayi sellam karanne naehae. (Children do not play.)
Egollo thuva:la venne naehae. (They are not injured.)

Lamai sellam karanne naethi hindha: egollo thuva:la venne naehae .
(Because children do not play, they are not injured.)

The only thing is to use your common sense when constructing sentences (this also applies to English and any other language for that matter). For example, you cannot make a complex sentence as follows even in English. Right?

Because I will study hard, I passed the exam.

Here, the cause and effect is reversed, and therefore the meaning is illogical and even funny. Just thinking that you can construct any sentence by rigidly following a set of rules is grossly wrong; there has to be a logical meaning in the constructed sentence too (use common sense).

Eya: haemathissema sindhu kiya kiya innava: .
(She is always singing.)
Eya: ho'ndha ga:yakayek ve:vi.
(She will become a good singer.)

Eya: haemathissema sindhu kiya kiya inna nisa: eya: ho'ndha ga:yakayek ve:vi.
(Because she is always singing, she will become a good singer.)

Eya: haemathissema sindhu kiyamin inna nisa: eya: ho'ndha ga:yakayek ve:vidha?
(Will she become a good singer because she is always singing?)

Eya: haemathissema sindhu kiya kiya hitiya: . (She was always singing.)

Eya: ho'ndha ga:yakayek ve:vi. (She will become a good singer.)

Eya: haemathissema sindhu kiya kiya hitapu/siti nisa: eya: ho'ndha ga:yakayek ve:vi.
(Because she was always singing, she will become a good singer.)

Eya: haemathissema sindhu kiyamin hitapu/siti nisa: eya: ho'ndha ga:yakayek vune: naedhdha?
(Didn't she become a good singer because she was always singing?)

Api vaththa pirisidhu karala: thiyenava: . (We have cleaned the garden.)
Madhuruvo bo:venne: naehae. (Mosquitoes do not breed.)

Api vaththa pirisidhu karala: thiyena nisa: madhuruvo bo:venne: naehae.
(Because we have cleaned the garden, mosquitoes do not breed.)

Api vaththa ho'ndhin pirisidhu kale: naethi nisa: madhuruvo bo: vuna: .
(Because we did not clean the garden well, mosquitoes bred.)

If the subject is same in both clauses, then you may omit the subject in the subsequent clause.

Eya: haemathissema sindhu kiya kiya inna nisa: eya: ho'ndha ga:yakayek ve:vi.

Eya: haemathissema sindhu kiya kiya inna nisa: ~~eya:~~ ho'ndha ga:yakayek ve:vi.

(Because she is always singing, she will become a good singer.)

Amma: uyana nisa: ~~eya:ta~~ TV balanna baehae.

(Because the mother is cooking, she can't watch TV.)

2. Vita, Kota, Gaman, -hama

– while/when/as

You generally follow the same set of rules described above. However, there are special points here. First, you do not use "-pu" verb form in this case. Secondly, in every time (present, past, future), you use the same verb form in the subordinate clause.

Lamaya: a'ndana kota, amma:th a'ndanava: .

(When the child cries, the mother too cries.)

Lamaya: a'ndana kota, amma:ath ae'nduva: .

(When the child cried, the mother too cried.)

Lamaya: a'ndanne: naethi vita, amma: a'nda:vidha?

(When the child does not cry, will the mother cry?)

Note:

In Sinhala you append *"-th"* to a noun to get the meaning of *"too/also"*· For example,

amma:th – *the mother too*

mamath – *I/me too*

oya:th – *you too*

balla:th – *the dog too*

minissuth – *men too or the men too (there is no definite-indefinite difference in plural in Sinhala)*

And when the noun ends with a consonant sound, then *"-uth"* is used instead·

ballekuth – *a dog too*

gahakuth – *a tree too*

bus ekakuth – *a bus too*

Sherinuth – *Sherin too*

When a noun is suffixed with prepositional modifier, then, *"-th"* suffix is put even after that·

amma:gen (from the mother) → ***amma:genuth*** *(from the mother too)*

ahase: (in the sky) → ***ahase:th*** *(in the sky too)*

Amma: uyamin inna gaman, ~~eya:~~ TV balanava: .
(While the mother is cooking, she is watching TV.)

Oya: pa:dam karanne naethi vita, sindhu ahanna.
(When you do not study, listen to songs/music.)

"gaman" is not used in negative subordinate clauses.

"-hama" is suffixed to the verb of the subordinate clause. Before suffixing it, you modify that verb a little bit. You change the verb into its past tense form first.

balanava:, baeluva: → *(baeluva:)* → ***baeluva:hama***
karanava:, keruva:/kala: → *(keruva:, kala:)* →
keruva:hama, kala:hama

Eya: man dhiha: baeluva:hama, mata a:daraya hithuna: .
(When she looked at me, I felt love.)

Eya: man dhiha baeluva:hama, mata a:daraya hithenava: .
(When she looks at me, I feel love.)

3. Nam, -hoth/-oth

– if/provided that/in case that

When using "nam", you simply put it after the subordinate clause with no modification to the verb.

> **Oya: gedhara yanava: nam, me:kath geniyanna.**
> (If you go home, take this too.)

> **Oya: eya:va dhaekka: nam, aeyi katha: kale: naeththe:?**
> (If you saw her, why did you not talk?)

> **Eya: oya:va dhaekke: naethi nam, baya venna epa:.**
> (If she did not see you, don't be afraid.)

"-oth/-hoth" is not used in past time. When using "-oth", it is appended to the tense verb, and the verb form is always the past time form and the ending vowel is dropped. When using "-hoth", it is appended to the tense verb, and the verb form is again the past time form, and now the long ending vowel is shortened.

> *balanava:* → *(baeluva:)* → **baeluvoth, baeluvahoth**
> *gahanava:* → *(gaehuva:)* → **gaehuvoth, gaehuvahoth**
> *karanava:* → *(kala:)* → **kaloth, kalahoth**
> *venava:* → *(vuna:)* → **vunoth, vunahoth**
> *kanava:* → *(kae:va:)* → **kae:voth, kae:vahoth**
> *dhenava:* → *(dhunna:)* → **dhunnoth, dhunnahoth**

Oya: gedhara giyoth me:kath geniyanna.
(If you go home, take this too.)

**Mata geyak thibboth oya: ma:va kasa:dha
badhinava:dha?**
(If I have a house, Will you marry me?)

Note:

To say somebody/something has or possesses
something, we use the Sinhala verb "*thiyenava:*".
Then, the subject (the person/thing that possesses)
is appended "-ta" in Sinhala. In the past time, it is
"*thibuna:*"; and in the future tense, it is "*thiye:vi*".
The negative form is "*naehae*" (present),
"*thibbe/thibune naehae*" (past), "*thiyena ekak
naehae*" (future).

> *Eya:ta geyak thiyenava:* .
>
> (He has a house.)
>
> *Eya:ta geyak thibuna:* .
>
> (He had a house)

Eya:ta geyak thiyenava:dha?

(Does he have a house?)

Eya:ta geyak thibuna:dha?

(Did he have a house?)

Mata car ekak thiyenava: ·

(I have a car·)

Mata car ekak thiye:vi·

(I will have a car)

Mata car ekak naehae·

(I don't have a car·)

Mata car ekak thibune: naehae·

(I did not have a car·)

Sheelata computer ekak thiyenava: ·

(Sheela has a computer·)

Sheelata computer ekak thiyenna o:na·

(Sheela should have a computer·)

And, when the object/complement after "*thiyenava:*"
or "*thibuna:*" or "*thiye:vi*" is animate/living, then we
must use "*innava:*", "*hitiya:*" or "*hi'ndhi:vi*"
respectively instead· Don't take these verbs in the
usual meaning of "stay/stayed/will stay" then· The
negative form is "*naehae*" (present), "*hitiye: naehae*"
(past), "*inna ekak naehae*" (future)·

> *Mata ballek innava:*
>
> (I have a dog·)

> *Mata ballek naehae·*
>
> (I do not have a dog·)

> *Mata ballek innava:dha?*
>
> (Do I have a dog?)

> *Mata ballek naethidha/naedhdha?*
>
> (Don't I have a dog?)

> *Sheelata kollek innava:* ·
>
> (Sheela has a boyfriend·)

Sheelata kollek hitiya: ·

(Sheela had a boyfriend·)

Sheelata kollek hitiya:dha?

(Did sheela have a boyfriend?)

Sheelata kollek hitiye naehae·

(Sheel did not have a boyfriend·)

Eya:ta kellek hi'ndhi:vi·

(He will have a girlfriend·)

Eya:ta kellek inna ekak naehae·

(He will not have a girlfriend·)

There are some more verbs like "*thiyenava:/innava:*
(have)" that requires appending "-ta" to the
subject/doer· These verbs are:

   hithenava: (think without efforts, feel)
   duka hithenava: (feel sad)
   sathutu hithenava: (feel happy)
You can construct verbs like the two examples above
by putting some adjective (which describes some

emotion) after "*hithenava:*"· And all of those forms
will behave in the same manner· The same principle
applies to the following case ("*dhaenenava:*") and
many other occasions too·

     dhaenenava: (feel)
     sathutu dhaenenava: (feel happy)
     duka dhaenenava: (feel sad)

     mathak/sihi venava: (remember)
     hina: yanava: (laugh)
     ke:nthi yanava: (get angry, go mad)
     nindha yanava: (fall asleep)
     kivisum yanava: (sneeze)

     Mata eya: gaena dhuka hithenava: ·
     (I feel sad about him·)

     Tha:ththata ikmanin ke:nthi yanava: ·
     (The father gets angry quickly·)

There may be more verbs behaving like above, and

when you practice the language, you will find easy and comfortable·

There is an interesting property in conjunctions that are appended to the verb of the subordinate clause. That is, when you make the subordinate clause negative, you prefix "no-" to the verb of the subordinate clause. See the following examples.

> **Mata geyak nothibboth, oya: ma:va kasa:dha badhinne: naedhdha?**
> (If I do not have a house, don't/won't you marry me?)

> **Eya: e:ka pass novunoth, ~~eya:ta~~ job eka laebena ekak naedhdha?**
> (If he does not pass the exam, won't he get the job.)

Actually, this method (of prefixing "no-") may be used with other conjunctions which are not suffixes to the verb as well.

> **Mata geyak nothibba: nam, oya: ma:va kasa:dha badhinava:dha?**
> (If I did not have a house, do/will you marry me?)

> **Eya: aeththa nokiyanava: nam, kohomadha mama eya:va visva:sa karanne:?**
> (If he does not tell the truth, how do I trust him?)

> **Eya: aeththa nokiyanava: nam, kohomadha mata eya:va visva:sa karanna puluvan?**
> (If he does not tell the truth, how can I trust him?)

4. "-ath"

– although/though/even though/even if

"-ath" is not used in past time (in the subordinate clause). It is appended to the tense verb of the subordinate clause, and the verb form is always in the past time <u>form</u> and the ending vowel is dropped.

karanava: → *(kala:)* → **kalath**
sellam karanava: → *(sellam kala:)* → **sellam kalath**
call karanava: → *(call kala:)* → **call kalath**

dhakinava: → *(dhaekka:)* → **dhaekkath**
venava: → *(vuna:)* → **vunath**

yanava: → *(giya:)* → **giyath**
kanava: → *(kae:va:)* → **kae:vath**
bonava: → *(bivva:)* → **bivvath**
dhenava: → *(dhunna:)* → **dhunnath**

Oya: e:ka kivvath mama oya: ekka tharaha naehae.
(I am not angry with you even if you tell it.)
(I am not angry with you even if you told it.)

Oya: giyath mama pa:dam karanava: .
(Though you go, I will study.)

Mata mahansi vunath ~~mama~~ e:ka ivara karanava: .
(Even though I am tired, I will finish it.)

Api haemada:ma katha: kara kara hitiyath, ~~api~~ ho'ndha ya:luvo neme: .

(Even if we were/are talking/chatting everyday, we are not good friends.)

Mama ho'ndhin pa:dam nokalath ~~mama~~ viba:gaya pass una: .

(Even if I did not study well, I passed the exam.)

5. Pera, Issella

– before

Here, the verb in the subordinate clause takes the form of infinitive (that is "-nna", "-nda", "-nnata"). In Sinhala, the subordinate clause has no difference in time (same for all 3 times).

Eya: enna/ennata/enda pera/issella man yanava: .
(Before he comes, I go.)

Eya: enna issella man giye:/giya: .
(I went before he came.)

Eya: enna issella man ya:vi.
(I will go before he comes.)

6. Pasu , Passe

– after

Here, the verb is always in the past tense form, and this past tense verb is also appended "-ta". The subordinate clause has no difference in time.

Eya: a:va:ta pasu/passe mama yanava: .
(After he comes, I go.)

Eya: a:va:ta passe mama giye:/giya: .
(After he came, I went.)

Eya: a:va:ta passe mama ya:vi/yanava: .
(After he comes, I will go.)

7. Eke:

- now that

The verb in the subordinate clause must be in the "-pu" form.

Oya: a:pu eke:, adha mehe: navathinna.
(Now that you came, stay here today.)

Eya: e:ka kana eke:, oyatath kanna puluvan baya naethiva.
(Now that he eats it, you too can eat it without fear.)

You may put the emphasizer suffix "-ma" to conjunctions. In English, you use "just" for that.

> **Oya: ena nisa:ma/hindha:ma man adha lassanata adhinava: .**
> (Just because you come, I wear beautifully today.)

> **Eya: kanna isselama, man kae:va: .**
> (Just before he ate, I ate.)

> **Api TV bala bala inna kotama, current giya: .**
> (Just while we were watching TV, electricity/power went off). (That is, there was a power cut.)

In English, you have "once" to give the meaning "just when"; and in Sinhala we have "**gamanma**" (gaman+ma) for that.

> **Oya: gedharata giya gamanma mata call ekak dhenna.**
> (Once you go home, give me a call.)

Now let us learn how to use the other category of conjunctions (*and, but, or*), which make compound sentences. However, in Sinhala it is a little bit more complicated than in English. Therefore, I will explain Sinhala compound sentences and some related/incidental matters in a few sections in terms of English ones.

Uses of "And", "But" and "Or"

1. In English, you use comma and "and" to join nouns, adjectives, adverbs, preposition (I am excluding the verb from this section for a very good reason). In Sinhala, you use the same method, and the equivalent Sinhala word for "and" is

"saha" or *"ha:"*.

> **Sherin, Sheela, Doris, ha:/saha Nita** *(Sherin, Sheela, Doris, and Nita)*

> **usa, mahatha, ha lassana lamaya:** *(the tall, fat, and beautiful child)*

> **ikmanin, ha lassanata liyanava:** *(write quickly, and beautifully)*
>
> **me:saya uda ha vate:ta** *(on and around the table)*

2. You can use "and" to join verbs in English just as you did with other types of words described in the first section. However, in Sinhala, it is different. You do not use comma or "saha/ha:" with verbs. Instead, there is a different method. Let us learn it now.

Each verb except the last verb (in the list of verbs/verb phrases) is converted to "-la:" form. The "-la:" verb is constructed by removing "nava:" from the original "-nava: verb" and appending "-la" to it. There are a few exceptions in the usual pattern too (I have listed some/most of them).

*karanava: → **karala:***
*balanava: → **balala:***
*natanava: → **natala:***
*venava: → **vela:***

*kanava: → **ka:la:***
*bonava: → **bi:la:***
*yanava: → **gihilla:***
*enava: → **aevilla:***
*dhenava: → **dhi:la:***
*ge:nava: (bring) → **genaella:***

The mother cooks, and eats.
Amma: uyala: kanava: .

The mother cooks, eats, and drinks.
Amma: uyala: ka:la: bonava: .

All above examples are just single verbs (verb participles).
However, you know the rights of a verb (ability to possess
adverbs, objects/complements, preposition parts) now. Therefore,
you can construct verb phrases as follows too.

The mother cooks rice, and eats quickly.
Amma: bath uyala: ikmanin kanava: .

*The mother cooks rice, eats quickly, and drinks water
slowly.*
**Amma: bath uyala: ikmanin ka:la: vathura semin
bonava: .**

Mama potha kiyavala: e:ka kiyannadha?
(Shall I read the book and tell it (then)?)
Nancy liyuma kiyavala: ae'nduva: .
(Nancy read the letter, and cried.)

Api heta udhe: ka:la: ehe: yanava: .
(We will eat and go there tomorrow morning.)

3. In English, you can join two or more sentences with "and". In Sinhala too, you can do the same. If you want to translate such an English compound sentence, you may translate clauses in the compound sentence individually disregarding "and" there.

> *The mother is cooking, and the father is reading the newspaper.*
> **Amma: uyanava: (or uyamin innava:) . Tha:ththa: paththaraya kiyavanava: (or kiyavamin innava:).**

Optionally, you may put an adverb "*e: athare:*" between the two individual sentences/clauses (that is, the second sentence starts with "*e: athare:*"). Still two or several sentences are there.

> *The mother is cooking, and the father is reading the newspaper.*
> **Amma: uyanava: (or uyamin innava:) . E: athare: tha:ththa: paththaraya kiyavanava: (or kiyavamin innava:).**

Or else, you may optionally put a Sinhala conjunction "*athare:*" between the two individual clauses, and now there is only one big compound sentence.

The mother is cooking, and the father is reading the newspaper.

Amma: uyana(or uyamin inna) athare: tha:ththa: paththaraya kiyavanava: (or kiyavamin innava:).

In above cases, the verb of the first clause is modified – "va:" part is removed from the "- nava:" verb in the present time; in the past time, you should use "-pu" verb form instead. Also note that in the past tense, you can still use the present time form.

The mother was cooking, and the father was reading the newspaper.

Amma: uya uya hitiya: (or ivva:) . Tha:ththa: paththaraya kiyavamin hitiya: (or kiyevva:).

Amma: uyamin hitiya: (or ivva:). E: athare: tha:ththa: paththaraya kiyavamin hitiya: (or kiyevva:)

Amma: uyamin hitapu (or uyapu) athare: tha:ththa: paththaraya kiyavamin hitiya: (or kiyevva:).

Amma: uyamin inna (or uyana) athare: tha:ththa: paththaraya kiyavamin hitiya: (or kiyevva:).

4. For English "but", Sinhala has the equivalent

"namuth" or *"eheth"*

(actually, *"eheth"* is similar to "however", but just as English speakers use "but" in places where "however" should be used, Sinhala speakers too do the same).

Here, the verb in the first clause (before the "but") is modified as in section 3 above. The "va:" part is removed from the present time "-nava:" verb. In the past time, "-pu" verb is used.

I am eating rice, but the mother is eating bread.
Mama bath kamin inna namuth amma: pa:n kamin innava: .

Peter listened to the radio, but Nancy watched TV.
Peter radio ekata ahumkan dhunna namuth Nancy TV baeluva: .

5. English "or" actually has several meanings/usages. In one usage, it shows two alternatives. These alternatives may be nouns, adjectives, adverbs, prepositions (I exclude verbs from this list). In this sense, Sinhala uses

"ho:".

Anne ho: Rita
(Anne or Rita)

rathu ho: kola shirt eka ganna.
(Take the red or green shirt.)

ikmanin ho: lassanata liyanna.
(Write quickly or beautifully.)

me:saya udin ho: yatin potha thiyanna.
(Put the book on or under the table.)

Optionally there is another popular pattern; actually this is equivalent to English pattern "**either...or...**". Here, the Sinhala pattern is *"**ekko: ... naethinam ...**"*. You put the two words in

the two blanks. In case of prepositions, you may optionally put
"*ekko:*" even before the noun connected to the preposition.

> ***ekko: Anne: naethinam Rita***
> *(either Anne or Rita)*

> **ekko: rathu naethinam kola shirt eka ganna.**
> (Take either the red or green shirt.)

> **ekko: ikmanin naethinam lassanata liyanna.**
> (Write either quickly or beautifully.)

> **me:saya ekko: udin naethinam yatin potha thiyanna.**
> **ekko: me:saya udin naethinam yatin potha thiyanna.**
> (Put the book either on or under the table.)

6. Sometimes you want to refer to the same person/thing in
different names, nouns, capacities, designations, etc. In English,
"or" (in the sense of *"also known as"*) is used for this usage too,
but in Sinhala

"hevath" or "nohoth"

is used.

> **William hevath/nohoth Willy**
> *(William or/also known as Willy)*

> ***polova hevath/nohoth nil grahaya:***
> *(the Earth or/also known as the blue planet)*

> ***Martin hevath yakada miniha:*** *(Martin or the iron man)*

7. In giving commands, you can give alternatives (*"do this or do that"*). In Sinhala, we use the same pattern as we saw in section 5 above (*"ekko: ... naethinam ..."*).

ekko: satan karanna naethinam dhuvanna.
(Fight or flight) (either fight or flight)

ekko: me:ka kanna naethinam maerenna.
(Eat this or die.)

8. You can use "or" to join two sentences in the sense that " *'you do this* (a command)' or else *'something else will happen* (a consequence)' ". In Sinhala too, we have this same pattern. Here, you just say a simple sentence (*"you do this"* type of sentence), and then put *"**naethinam**"* and after that you say the other *"something else will happen"* type sentence.

Oya: kanna naethinam ~~oya:~~ maerevi.
(You eat or else you will die.)

Oya: yanna naethinam eya:ta dhuka hithe:vi.
(You go or else she will feel sad.)

Relative Pronouns and Reported Speech in Sinhala

There are two other methods of joining two sentences.

1. English sentences using **relative pronouns** (*who, whom, which, that*).

Actually, this sentence pattern is already covered. Do you remember how you constructed the following type of Sinhala sentences?

> **Ge:ttuva la'nga a'ndamin inna lamaya: mage: nangi:.**
> (The girl who is crying at the gate is my younger sister.)

2. Reported speech & *"'that' clauses"*

In English, you join two sentences with *"that"* or some other equivalent connective word (whether, if, wh-word) having the same effect (see the examples). We are going to construct Sinhala sentences for the following types of English sentences.

Josh said that he did it.
Jane asked if/whether you did it.
Joseph wants to know what you did really.

It is very easy to make these types of sentences in Sinhala. You have to follow the same pattern for all these three types (English had 3 structures, but Sinhala has only one structure for them all).

You just say the both clauses in usual ways, and put/say *"**kiyala**"* after the *"that clause"*. That's it.

Josh kivva:.

(Josh said.)

Eya: e:ka kala: → **Eya: e:ka kala: kiyala:**

(He did it.)　　　(that he did it.)

Josh kivva: eya: e:ka kala: kiyala.

(Josh said that he did it.)

Josh kivva: eya: e:ka kale: naehae kiyala.

(Josh said that he did not do it.)

Josh kiyanava: eya: e:ka karanava: kiyala.

(Josh says he will do it.)

Jane aehuva: oya: e:ka kala:dha kiyala.

(Jane asked if you did it.)

Jane ahanava oya: e:ka kale: naedhdha kiyala.

(Jane asked if you did not do it.)

Josephta dhaena ganna o:na oya: mokakdha kale: kiyala.

(Joseph wants to know what you did.)

Numbers in Sinhala

Let us learn how to work with **numbers** now. First, memorize the following Sinhala words/sounds for numbers. There are nice and easy patterns just like in English. Only *"eka siyaya"* is slightly different because instead of "ek-", it has *"eka"* (but still "ek-" in prefix form is as same as *"eka"* both having the meaning of "one").

1 - **eka**	2 - **dheka**	3 - **thuna**
4 - **hathara**	5 - **paha**	6 - **haya**
7 - **hatha**	8 - **ata**	9 – **navaya**
10 - **dhahaya**	11 - **ekolaha**	12 - **dholaha**
13 - **dhahathuna**	14 - **dhahahathara**	15 - **pahalava**
16 - **dhahasaya**	17 - **dhahahatha**	18 – **dhaha-ata**
19 - **dhahanavaya**	20 – **vissa** (*"visi-"*)	21 – visi-eka
22 – visi-dheka	23 – visi-thuna	24 – visi-hathara
25 – visi-paha	26 – visi-haya	27 – visi-hatha
28 – visi-ata	29 – visi-navaya	30 – **thiha** (*"this-"*)
31 – this-eka	32 – this-dheka	33 – this-thuna etc
40 – **hathaliha** (*"hathalis-"*)	41 – hathalis-eka	42 – hathalis-dheka etc
50 – **panaha** (*"panas-"*)	60 – **haeta** (*"haeta-"*)	70 – **haeththae:va** (*"haeththae:-"*)
80 – **asu:va** (*"asu:-"*)	90 – **anu:va** (*"anu:-"*)	100 – **eka** *siyaya* (*"eka siya-"*)

101 – eka siya eka	110 – eka siya dhahaya	162 – eka siya haeta dheka
200 – **dhe**siyaya ("dhesiya-")	300 – **thun**siyaya ("thunsiya-")	400 – **ha:ra**siyaya ("ha:rasiya-")
500 – **pan**siyaya ("pansiya-") etc	600 – **haya**siyaya	700 – **hath**siyaya
800 – **ata**siyaya	900 - **nava**siyaya	1000 – **ek**dhaha ("ekdhahas-")
1001 – ekdhahas eka	1031 – ekdhahas this-eka	1421 – ekdhahas ha:rasiya visi-eka
2000 – **dhe**dhaha ("dhedhahas-")	3000 – **thun**dhaha ("thundhahas-")	4000 – **ha:ra**dhaha
5000 - **pan**dhaha	6000 - **haya**dhaha	7000 - **hath**dhaha
8000 - **ata**dhaha	9000 - **nava**dhaha	10,000 – **dhas**adhaha/**dhaha**dhaha
11,000 – **ekolos**dhaha	12,000 - **dholos**dhaha	13,000 - **dhahathun**dhaha
14,000 - **dhahahathara**dhaha	15,000 - **pahalos**dhaha	16,000 - **dhahasaya**dhaha
17,000 - **dhahahath**dhaha	18,000 – **dhaha-ata**dhaha	19,000 - **dhahanavaya**dhaha
20,000 - **visi**dhaha	30,000 – **this**dhaha etc	85,126 – asu:pandhahas ekasiya visi-haya
100,000 – **eklakshaya** ("eklaksha-")	100,001 – eklaksha eka	100,088 – eklaksha asu:ata
100,312 – eklaksha thunsiya dholaha	104,000 – eklaksha	151,658 – eklaksha panas ekdhahas hayasiya panas

	ha:radhaha	ata
200,000 - **dhe**lakshaya	300,000 - **thun**lakshaya	400,000 – **ha:ra**lakshaya etc
10,00,000 – **dhasa**lakshaya	10,02,155 – dhasalaksha dhedhahas ekasiya panas paha	20,00,000 – **visi**lakshaya etc
100,00,000 – **ekko:tiya** ("ekko:ti-")	10,000,000,000 – siya ko:tiya	0 - bindhuva

In Sinhala, *dhasalaksaya* is not a special number that has its own unique name, but in English, it gets its own special name "million". Therefore, if you like, you can use "*miliyanaya*" (the Sinhalized version of "million"). Likewise you may use "*biliyanaya*" instead of "siyako:tiya. Therefore, you may use English numbers like trillion ("*triliyanaya*") for higher values.

As you have noticed, each number has a prefix form too. You can understand it from the above table, but I will list them below for further clarity.

ek- (1, like uni- in English)	dhe- (2)	thun- (3)
hathara- (4)	pas- (5)	haya- (6)
hath- (7)	ata- (8)	nava- (9)
Dhasa- , dhaha (10)	Ekolos- (11)	Dholos- (12)
Dhahathun- (13)	Dhahahathara- (14)	Pahalos- (15)
Dhahasaya- (16)	Dhahath- (17)	Dhaha-ata- (18)
Dhahanava- (19)	Visi- (20)	Visi-ek- (21)
Visi-dhe- (22)	Visi-hath- (27) etc	This- (30) etc

Eksiya- (100)	Eksiya panas-thun- (153) etc	Dhesiya- (200) etc
Ekdhahas- (1000)	Ekdhahas thunsiya panas- (1350) etc	Hathdhahas- (7000) etc
Eklaksha- (100,000) etc	Thunko:ti- (300,00,000)	

You can use numbers in Sinhala as nouns or adjectives. After a plural <u>inanimate</u> noun, you may put a number. Automatically, it would be a definite noun. If you want to make the noun indefinite you must append "-**ak**" ("-k") suffix to the number (not to the noun).

> ***Bo:la paha*** *– the five balls (definite)*
> ***Bo:la pahak*** *– five balls (indefinite)*

> ***Pae:n thuna*** *– the three pens*
> ***Pae:n thunak*** *– three pens*

> ***Poth dhesiyaya*** *– the 200 books*
> ***Poth dhesiyayak*** *– 200 books*

After a plural <u>animate</u> noun, you usually use the related numeral prefix as described and shown in the above table with "***dhena:***" (if definite) or with "***dhenek***" (if indefinite).

> ***Lamayin pas dhena:*** *(the five children)*
> ***Lamayin pas dhenek*** *(five children)*

> ***Ballo: thun dhena:*** *(the three dogs)*
> ***Ballo: thun dhenek*** *(three dogs)*

> ***Driverla dhesiya dhena:*** *(the 200 drivers)*
> ***Driverla dhesiya dhenek*** *(200 drivers)*

Sometimes, you may use the same method that you use for inanimate nouns for animate nouns too (especially for animals).

> ***Pu:san atak*** *(eight cats)*

Let us learn how to say **fractions** (*"ba:ga sankya:"*) and **decimal numbers** (*"dashama sankya:"*) in Sinhala. It is as easy as in English. The number above is called the *"lavaya"* (numerator) and the number below is the *"haraya"* (denominator) of a fraction (for example, in ¾, 3 is numerator and 4 is denominator). We first say the denominator and then say the numerator. And you append "**-en**" suffix (which means "from") to the denominator too.

> ¼ - ***hatharen eka*** *(or "ka:la")*
> ¾ - ***hatharen thuna*** *(or "thunka:la")*
> ½ - ***dheken eka*** *(or "ba:gaya")*
> 1/8 – ***aten eka*** *(or "harikka:la")*
> 2/3 –***thunen dheka***

Let us put these fractions in context now.

> ***Vathura thunen dheka*** *(the two-thirds of water)*
> ***Vathura thunen dhekak*** *(two-thirds of water)*
>
> ***Pa:n hatharen eka (or ka:la)*** *(the one-fourth of bread)*
> ***Pa:n hatharen ekak (or ka:lak)*** *(a one-fourth of bread)*

How to pronounce a decimal number? You first say the whole number part, then say "***dhasama***", and finally say each digit in the decimal part. And you append "-**yi**" to the whole number and each digit.

12.346 – dholahayi dhasama thunayi hatharayi hayayi

461.1270 – ha:rasiya haeta ekayi dhasama ekai dhekai hathayi bindhuvayi.

You must also learn how to say numbers in the style of "first", "second", "third", "fourth", etc (ordinal numbers). It is very easy to make them by adding "*vaeni*" after a prefix form number. "first" is an exception; it has its own name/sound.

Palavaeni, palamuvaeni – 1st	Dhevaeni – 2nd	Thunvaeni – 3rd
Hatharavaeni – 4th	Pasvaeni – 5th	Hayavaeni – 6th
Hathvaeni – 7th	Atavaeni – 8th	Navavaeni – 9th
Dhahavaeni, dhasavaeni – 10th	Ekolosvaeni – 11th etc	Visivaeni – 20th etc
Ekasiyavaeni – 100th	Ekasiya ekvaeni – 101st	Dhesiya panas thunvaeni – 253rd
Ekdhahasvaeni – 1000th etc	**Panlakshaya**vaeni – 500,000th	**Ko:tiya**vaeni – 100,00,000th

These ordinal numbers are used as normal adjectives with nouns.

Thunvaeni potha ge:nna.

(Bring the third book.)

Mama ekasiya atavaeni namata kaemathiy.

(I like the 108th name.)

You can also make an adverb with numeral prefixes too. Just prefix them to *"pa:rak"* or *"saerayak"*. In English, you do this with *"times"*.

> **Ekpa:rak, eksaerayak** – one time (once)
> **dhepa:rak, dhesaerayak** – two times (twice)
> **thunpa:rak, thunsaerayak** – three times
> **siyapa:rak, siyasaerayak** – hundred times
>
> **Man eya:ta passaerayak call kala: .**
> (I called him five times.)

Now let us see some miscellaneous Sinhala usages to finish this series of lessons.

Impersonal Pronoun

In English, you use "you" as an impersonal pronoun when you want to say something impersonally. For example:

You should not kill animals.

Even if "you" is there as the subject, it in fact means "anyone". Sometimes "one" is used instead in English of course. We had to use "you" or "one" because there is no specific subject there but it is mandatory to use a subject in English sentences.

However, Sinhala is much simpler here because spoken Sinhala does not require a subject (or even an object) to construct a sentence. Therefore, you can express this type of sentences in Sinhala one of two ways.

One way is to say it as a command (this is exactly when you use "you" in English too). Usually, the English helping verbs in negative form - *shouldn't, mustn't, shan't, oughtn't to*, are treated as "*epa:* (don't)" or "*ho'ndha naehae* (not good)".

> **Sathun maranna epa: .**
> (You don't kill animals.)
>
> **Sathun maeriya yuthu naehae.**
> **Sathun maranna ho'ndha naehae.**
> (You shouldn't kill animals.)

The other way that is more interesting is to express it as a normal sentence without a subject (this is when you use "one" in English).

Me: ka:le job ekak laba:ganna puluvan.

(These days one can get a job.)

E:ka kanna puluvan.

(You/One can eat it.)

How to say this following type of sentence in Sinhala?

"hey Bob, what are you doing?"

"I am just reading."

Here Bob is doing the act of "reading" because he has nothing important to do at the moment. In Sinhala, we use the adverb *"nikan"* or *"ohe:"* like we used "just" in English.

Man nikan kiyavanavamin innava: .

(I am just reading.)

Api ohe: katha: kara kara hitiya: .

(We were just talking.)

You may put *"ma:ra"* as an adverb in front of an adjective or another adverb, and it has the meaning of "very".

Eya: ma:ra lassanai.

(She is so/very beautiful.)

Eya: ma:ra lassanata liyanava.

(She writes so/very beautifully.)

Greetings in Sinhala

Let us see how to greet in Sinhala. In some occasions, English phrases are used too. You can wish (for anything) by putting "*suba*" (happy) in front of the occasion/day like "*suba upandhiyanak* (happy birthday)", "*suba naththalak* (happy Christmas)", etc.

Thank you, thanks, sthu:thiy, bohoma sthuthiy
(thank you)

Good morning, suba udhae:sanak
(good morning)

Good night, suba ra:thriyak
(good night)

Good evening/afternoon, suba sandhae:vak
(good evening/afternoon)

Sorry, excuse me, sama: venna
(sorry, excuse me)

Hello
(over the phone or when you meet somebody; same as in English)

Bye
(over the phone or when you leave; same as in English)

Passe hamuve mu, gihin ennam, see you
(see you)

Hi
(hello)

Kohomadha, kohomadha ithin, kohomadha saepa sani:pa
(how are you doing)

Suba upandhiyanak, suba upandhinayak ve:va:
(happy birthday)

Suba aluth avurudhdhak, suba aluth avurudhdhak ve:va:
(happy new year)

Ese:ma ve:va
(the same to you)

Congratulations, suba paethum
(congratulations)

Suba pathanava: , good luck, all the best
(Wish you good luck/success/etc, all the best)

"...va" mathak kala: kiyanna.
(give my regards to "...")

> **Sherinva mathak kala: kiyanna.**
> (Give my regards to Sherin.)

Interjections and Curse Words

Just as in any other language, Sinhala language too has many idiomatic expressions (such expressions that has entirely different meaning than its literal meaning), and figures of speech. After you learn the basics of grammar and obtain a good working vocabulary, you can learn them slowly. I am showing some of them.

Amma: palla:, dheviyan/dheyyan palla:
(cross my heart) (a swear word)

> **Amma: palla:, mama e:ka kivve: naehae.**
> (Cross my heart; I did not say it.)

Ammata siri, appata siri
(oh no, oh boy) (a surprise)

> **Ammata siri, oya: e:ka kala:dha?**
> (oh no, did you do it?)

Dheyyane:, amme:, appe:
(oh my god) (sad surprise)

> **Dheyyane:, balla: si:thale: maerila: .**
> (Oh my god, the dog has died of coldness.)

Pissu, vika:ra, mala vika:ra, payiththiyan
(bullshit, nonsense)

Vika:ra, man ehema kivve: naehae.
> (Nonsense, I did not say so.)

Sha:, niyamai, sha: niyamai, maru, sha: maru
(great, fantastic, excellent) (excitement)

Chik, shik, shit
(shit) (anger or contempt)

i:ya:
(say when you feel disgusting)

hena gahapiya, hena gahapan, maka bae:viyan
(go to hell)

mala vadhe:, va:thayak/va:the:, mala dha:ne
(pain in the butt)

magula, thuk, thuk vitharak
(damn it)

kamak/avlak/prasnayak naehae
(no problem)

"...ta" kamak naehae.
(it doesn't matter to "...")

   Mata kamak naehae eya: aeththa kivva:ta.
   (It doesn't matter to me if he tells/told the truth).
Usually you put a simple sentence that ends with a verb
in the form "*kivva:ta*" (in the past time) or "*kiyanava:ta*"
(in the present time).

karume:, mage: karume:
(just my luck)

This is the end of this series of lessons. I tried to teach spoken
Sinhala with grammar. Many books teaching Spoken Sinhala out

there lack solid grammatical underpinning and foundation. They just list thousands of phrases. You are supposed to memorize them like how a parrot does. I personally cannot imagine how you can express your own creative ideas then.

Read, Analyze (patterns), Learn, and memorize the material in the given order because later lessons are based on the previous ones. Good Luck!

Sinhala Alphabet and Writing

I will show you the Sinhala alphabet. I recommend learning it
too. There are 60 letters in the modern Sinhala alphabet. Even
though the following shows the standard forms/shapes of the
characters, when natives write them with hand, you have to
recognize the characters by their basic shape.

Vowels

Following picture shows the Sinhala **vowels**. Beside (in front of)
each letter is the name of the letter and below each letter is the
sound it represents. The first 12 vowels are very important.

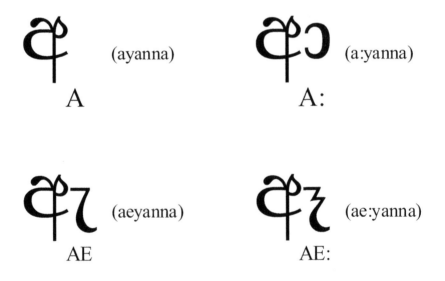

(ayanna)

A

(a:yanna)

A:

(aeyanna)

AE

(ae:yanna)

AE:

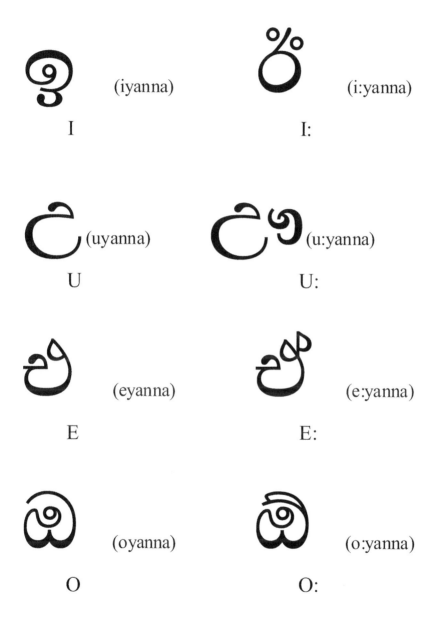

(iyanna)

I

(i:yanna)

I:

(uyanna)

U

(u:yanna)

U:

(eyanna)

E

(e:yanna)

E:

(oyanna)

O

(o:yanna)

O:

ඓ (ayyanna)
AY

ඖ (owuyanna)
AV

ඍ (iruyanna)
R

ඎ (iru:yanna)
R

Consonants

The following picture shows the **consonants** of Sinhala alphabet (not in the conventional order and format). In the first set of letters, you can see two columns of characters. The two letters in each row are almost same (there is only a subtle difference in pronunciation). Actually, you should remember all the letters, but I suggest you to use only the letters that are in the first column. The English sound of each letter is shown in front.

Kayanna   ක   K   ඛ

Gayanna   ග   G   ඝ

Chayanna	ච	CH	ඡ
Jayanna	ජ	J	ඣ
Tayanna	ට	T	ඨ
Dayanna	ඩ	D	ඪ
Thayanna	ත	TH	ථ
Dhayanna	ද	DH	ධ
Payanna	ප	P	ඵ
Bayanna	බ	B	භ

Nayanna	න	N	ඤ
Shayanna	ශ	SH	ඹ
Layanna	ල	L	ළ
Gnayanna	ඦ	NG	ඦ
Yayanna	ය	Y	
rayanna	ර	R	
vayanna	ව	V	

hayanna හ H

fayanna ෆ F

sa'gnaka gayanna ඟ 'ng

sa'gnaka dayanna ඬ 'nd

sa'gnaka dhayanna ඳ 'ndh

sa'gnaka bayanna ඹ 'nb

Sinhala alphabet is phonetic (that is, each letter shall have one dedicated sound only), therefore it is easier to use than English alphabet. Consonant letters cannot be sounded on their own, and you have to use vowels to aid in them to be pronounced. In English, you just place the vowel just after the consonant. For example:

$$K + A \rightarrow KA$$
$$T + O \rightarrow TO$$
$$N + OA = NOA$$

However, in Sinhala, you cannot use this method. Instead you use **diacritical marks** (called "*pillam*" or "*pili*" in Sinhala) to denote the vowel sound a consonant letter possesses.

Actually all the letters shown as in the above picture already have the vowel sound "a" in them (by standard, they are the *default letter* forms). The real consonant form must be shown by using a diacritical mark called "*kodiya*". After applying kodiya, the letters are called "*hal akuru*" (*akura* means letter, and *akuru* is the plural of akura). Applying a kodiya (to a default letter) is called "*halkaranava:*".

There are two forms of "*kodiya*", and I will list them all in the following table. To show clearly how this diacritical mark in both forms is applied on characters, I have enlarged the first cage in the table.

Sa'gnaka letters can never take a kodiya. In addition, bindhuva and visargaya too cannot take a kodiya (these two letters are natural "*hal akuru*", and cannot take any of diacritical marks).

ළු	ළ	ල	ඞ
ක	ඝ	ඨ	ඛ
ඥ	ඞ	ඥ	ඥ
	ඔ	ඕ	ඖ

Letter Combination

Now let us see how you write consonants aided with a vowel. For this, you have to use several types of *pillam* (I have written the names of all the pillam in bold below). For example:

ක් + අ = ක
(though ක has a vowel, it is considered as the default letter)

ක් + ආ = කා (this pillama is called the "**aelapilla**")

ක් + ඇ = කැ ("**aedhaya**" or "**aedhapilla**")

ක් + ඈ = කෑ ("**dhi:rga aedhaya**" or "**dhi:rga aedhapilla**")
                    ("dhi:rga" means "short".)

ක් + ඉ = කි ("**ispilla**")

ක් + ඊ = කී ("**dhi:rga ispilla**")

ක් + උ = කු , න් + උ = නු ("**pa:pilla**")

ක් + ඌ = කූ , න් + ඌ = නූ ("**dhi:rga pa:pilla**")

ක් + එ = ෙක ("**kombuva**")

ක් + ඒ = ෙකී ("**kombuva ha: kodiya**")

ක් + ඔ = ෙකා ("**kombuva ha: aelapilla**")

ක් + ඕ = ෙකෝ ("**kombuva ha: kodiya sahitha aelapilla**")

ක් + ෞ = කෞ ("kombu dheka")

ක් + ඔ = කෘ ("kombuva ha: **gayanukiththa**")

ක් + ා = කැ ("**aelapili gaetaya**")

ක් + ෑ = කෑ ("aelapili gaeta dheka")

As you can notice, each vowel has a pillama (some vowels have two pillams too). In the following table, I have listed all the Sinhala *consonant+vowel* combinations. Even if I have shown you all combinations, in practice you will not find some combinations (I have struck them out).

	ආ	ඇ	ඈ	ඉ	ඊ	උ	ඌ	එ	ඒ	ඔ	ඕ	ඓ	ඖ	සෘ	සෲ
ක්	කා	කැ	කෑ	කි	කී	කු	කූ	කෙ	කේ	කො	කෝ	කෛ	කෞ	කෘ	කෲ
ඛ්	ඛා	ඛැ	ඛෑ	ඛි	ඛී	ඛු	ඛූ	ඛෙ	ඛේ	ඛො	ඛෝ	ඛෛ	ඛෞ	~~ඛෘ~~	~~ඛෲ~~
ග්	ගා	ගැ	ගෑ	ගි	ගී	ගු	ගූ	ගෙ	ගේ	ගො	ගෝ	ගෛ	ගෞ	ගෘ	ගෲ
ඝ්	ඝා	ඝැ	ඝෑ	ඝි	ඝී	ඝු	ඝූ	ඝෙ	ඝේ	ඝො	ඝෝ	ඝෛ	ඝෞ	ඝෘ	ඝෲ

	ආ	ඇ	ඈ	ඉ	ඊ	උ	ඌ	එ	ඒ	ඔ	ඕ	ඓ	ඖ	සෘ	සෲ
ච්	චා	චැ	චෑ	චි	චී	චු	චූ	චෙ	චේ	චො	චෝ	චෛ	චෞ	~~චෘ~~	~~චෲ~~
ඡ්	ඡා	ඡැ	ඡෑ	ඡි	ඡී	ඡු	ඡූ	ඡෙ	ඡේ	ඡො	ඡෝ	ඡෛ	ඡෞ	~~ඡෘ~~	~~ඡෲ~~
ජ්	ජා	ජැ	ජෑ	ජි	ජී	ජු	ජූ	ජෙ	ජේ	ජො	ජෝ	ජෛ	ජෞ	~~ජෘ~~	~~ජෲ~~
ඣ්	ඣා	ඣැ	ඣෑ	ඣි	ඣී	ඣු	ඣූ	ඣෙ	ඣේ	ඣො	ඣෝ	ඣෛ	ඣෞ	~~ඣෘ~~	~~ඣෲ~~

	ආ	ඇ	ඈ	ඉ	ඊ	උ	ඌ	එ	ඒ	ඔ	ඕ	ඓ	ඖ	සෘ	සෲ
ට්	ටා	ටැ	ටෑ	ටි	ටී	ටු	ටූ	ටෙ	ටේ	ටො	ටෝ	ටෛ	ටෞ	ටෘ	ටෲ
ඨ්	ඨා	ඨැ	ඨෑ	ඨි	ඨී	ඨු	ඨූ	ඨෙ	ඨේ	ඨො	ඨෝ	ඨෛ	ඨෞ	~~ඨෘ~~	~~ඨෲ~~
ඩ්	ඩා	ඩැ	ඩෑ	ඩි	ඩී	ඩු	ඩූ	ඩෙ	ඩේ	ඩො	ඩෝ	ඩෛ	ඩෞ	ඩෘ	ඩෲ
ඪ්	ඪා	ඪැ	ඪෑ	ඪි	ඪී	ඪු	ඪූ	ඪෙ	ඪේ	ඪො	ඪෝ	ඪෛ	ඪෞ	~~ඪෘ~~	~~ඪෲ~~

You can read tons of text in Sinhala letters on the Internet. To read and write Sinhala letters, you must have a Sinhala font in Unicode standard. The Sinhala font "Iskolapotha" designed by Microsoft is perfect. All the modern operating systems in computers and smart phones now support Unicode standard, but most probably these devices may not render/show Sinhala though (instead, you will see a bunch of small boxes). The problem is that these devices have no Sinhala Unicode font installed on them yet (after installing one, you can work with Sinhala easily just as you would work with English or any other language for that matter). Due to some technical glitches, sometimes (mostly Windows operating systems) you may not be able to write Sinhala correctly. In that case, there are some simple fixes (installing a very tiny program) and you can google them.

I am currently writing another book to supplement this book with conversations and phrases in Sinhala. I am also planning to write some Sinhala storybooks (with English translation).

Printed in Great Britain
by Amazon

11493507R00130